MW00511047

Diana Love Story (PT. 3)

Graduation, and we plan to be a part of the season.

Tina Scott

Before I even went to the toilet, I got up and called Diana. She wanted to come to my place, and I told her to come over after 1:30, so I could rest, clean up, and get back to normal. After we finished talking, I went to the bathroom to shave and wash. When I was done, I felt ready to rejoin my kin. Camilla was at a friend's home, which was fortunate because it made it possible to speak to my parents without her there. When I told them about how bad things had been with Adrienne, they were really helpful, acknowledging that Ade had misbehaved. I was hoping it wouldn't jeopardize their relationship with Marvin and Sandy.

Then I mentioned the other issue that was worrying me. "Diana is at a sleepaway party like she does every season. It means we'd just see each other once a week, on her day off, assuming I would get the same day off. She asked if I wanted to work there for the summer, and although it sounds amazing, there are some drawbacks. First, I wouldn't see you and Camilla all summer, and then I'd just have about five days off before starting classes. Second, I'll earn somewhat less revenue, at least a thousand dollars less. And I promised Sy and Marilyn (the print shop owners) that I will work all summer to fund their holidays. I'm at a loss about what to do. Diana will be here at 1:30 to discuss this, and I'm at a loss for words."

My parents both reached for one of my palms, and that small touch conveyed a lot of affection and encouragement to me. I'd always been willing to speak to them and bring some problems to them. I was very fortunate because I met some of my peers who hardly spoke to their parents at all. My father talked on their behalf. "Forget about your promise to Sy and Marilyn, Jon. Don't even think about sharing time with us. Do you believe that not having Diana will be detrimental to your relationship? I'm talking around seeing her once a week or less."

"It couldn't be useful for it. Yet, I trust her in the same way she trusted me with Adrienne. She won't end up in a summer romance, and neither will I."

"And so you'll spend much of your spare time at school together, right? But it's summertime. I understand that eight weeks would seem like a long period. But if you believe you can do it, let her go. However, if you are compelled to spend the whole summer with her, go to work with her. We'll figure out the capital. We will assist you."

"No way, no how. You're always doing enough for me. And now that you're sick, you can preserve your resources anywhere you can."

That time, she responded. "Jon, a thousand dollars isn't going to make a difference in our lives. You are our baby, and we will do all in our power to assist you. I believe you can hold your promise to your boss. They've been kind to you over the past two years. But you must still do what is right for you, and only you know what it is."

It was entirely my choice. They weren't going to make that for me, which was the proper course of action. Diana and I had to work things out together. My parents, on the other hand, offer me, sound counsel.

Diana arrived on schedule, and after greeting my friends, we went upstairs to my room to chat privately. I just had to leave the door slightly ajar. It's your parent's home, and you have to follow your parent's laws.

I was the first to talk. "You did believe me last night, didn't you, honey? Were you concerned that I would not be loyal to you until I called?"

"No, it does not. No, not at all. I knew I could depend on you. I wasn't concerned in the least."

"That's how it is for me. I'm not worried that you'll find someone at camp who would break it up with me. And I'm not looking to find anybody here. What I mean is, Diana, I told my employers I'd be there this summer. They're relying on me. I would love to work at camp if it weren't for that, my vow to them. So it isn't really about wealth. I made a promise. Still, before we reach a definitive decision, let me ask you a question: Do you believe our friendship is good enough to be separated for the majority of the Summer?"

"Yes, I do. I'm not going to get entangled with anybody at camp, and I'm sure you won't either. So I'll miss you if I go. I'll miss my relatives more than anything else." Diana cradled me in her embrace and kissed me many times. "I adore you to the moon and beyond. It'll be difficult to be without you for the majority of the summer."

"The same thing happened to me. But after the summer is through, we'll have too much time to look forward to. We'll be together for the rest of the year. I don't say any of the time. We just need one cooperative, or mainly absent... roommate, and we'll spend so much time together that we'll learn to despise each other!" With a wide smile, I said.

"Never, ever! You're quite the character, last night proposing marriage and today discussing hating each other. For some couples, that equates to ten years." We embraced for a moment, rocking back and forth. We couldn't do much more with my parents in the kitchen. "Are you sure, Jon? If you like, I'll do something else for the summer, like the YMCA's day camp (the YM-YWHA). I realize we'll be fine in the end, but I don't want to be separated for too long." Her mouth teased mine as her hand rubbed across my jaw.

"I'm not going to tell you what you can do, honey. I can tell you that if you go, I'll miss you terribly. Yet I care so much for you that I trust you to do what's right for you. If you want to go to Surprise Lake (her camp), I suggest you go for it. It's not even that long, an hour and a half either way?"

"Yes, on the east side of the Hudson, just north of West Point. You'll pay us a call whenever you can?"

"You couldn't keep me safe, honey. As long as I can have the same days off each week, I'll be there every week. Please, darling, do this. I want you to do what brings you joy."

"If I did it right now, your parents would kick me out," Diana said with a lustful embrace. "Seriously, are you sure? I'd be leaving eight days after we graduated."

"Diana, hurry up!" With a grin, I said. "Consider how unique any time we see each other. We could only get a hotel room and shack up for the day."

"That is ideal! I wish we were alone right now just thinking about it." Several more kisses.

"That's nice because they'll be going grocery shopping shortly. Let's head downstairs for a few minutes. We should be able to be along shortly."

"Camilla, how are you? I don't want her to come home too soon."

"She'll be at a birthday party before 4 p.m. We'll have plenty of time if my parents left in the next hour."

While my mother was getting ready, we went downstairs and sat with my father. She was the sort of lady who never left the house without her makeup on. "You never know who you're going to meet," she used to say.

My father wanted me to assist him with everything in the garage, which was his code for speaking to me alone. He talked to me when we arrived. "I'm not going to advise you to 'behave' when we're out, Jon. I'm fairly sure I'm smarter than that. But keep in mind that your sister will be arriving home around 4 p.m. You must be presentable before she arrives. Also, please open your browser. I don't want the same thing to happen again."

It was a little embarrassing to speak about this openly with him, but I admired his honesty. "Dad, we'll be...respectful. I guarantee it. That's about what I have to think about it."

I went back inside, and he waited in the car for Mom. They were on their way to the store in five minutes, and Diana and I returned to my space after a respectful period.

"Did your father mention something to you in the garage?" she inquired. "However, I'm fairly certain I can guess the general subject."

"Are you sure you want to know?" She agreed with a smile. "He's fairly sure we're going to be together now, but no particulars have been provided, and he reminded me that Cammy will be home around 4 p.m. and that we should be, and I quote, 'presentable' by then. Sorry, you were curious."

Diana was flushed in the chest. "I think I knew they knew about us, like my parents, but it's always strange knowing they know...you know?" We both smiled as we kissed each other.

"I understand. I also realize Cammy will be home in a little more than an hour. Before then, I want to make sure my girlfriend is fully satisfied. I am overjoyed."

"Whatever we do, you make me happy, really happy. In your bed, your home, a gallery, or while dancing with you. I've never been happier in my life." Her wide brown eyes shone brightly. Then, teasingly, she unbuttoned her short-sleeved blouse, and I studied her, never moving my gaze away from her. She then reached behind her, and her bra fell loose, which she threw on the concrete. Diana licked her fingertips on both palms, closed her eyes, and sighed as she traced them across her areolas, allowing the moisture to shine through the lovely pink rings.

"Are you sure?" Diana said in a lustful whisper. Her eyes were just halfway wide. "If you like, you can prove it to me. In truth, I am adamant. Let me see how difficult you are for me, kid."

I got up in front of Diana, who was sitting on the edge of my bunk. I unbuttoned my jeans while she continued to play with her breasts, flicking them with her nails every few seconds, making her scream. Diana noticed how ready I was about her as I took off my denim cutoff shorts and briefs. I was fully stiff, all six inches of my groin and its gentle upward curve. "MMMMM," she moaned, then bent over and licked all over me, head and shaft, and it was my turn to moan.

9

"You're a naughty, naughty kid," I yelled as loudly as I could. "You should always get spanked for being such a poor kid."

"I believe you need some restraint, young lady. Get up and remove your pantyhose."

"We'll make it do more than a tingle, but first..." Diana leaned slightly over, reached under her short blacktop, and steadily pushed her panties down her thighs. I was almost drooling as I watched her. She understood how to make me laugh. She was getting pretty good at it.

Diana sat on my lap, her sweet, round butt poking up in the air just enough for her to feel me on her tummy but not so far that she pressed down so tightly on me. I took my right hand and stroked her lower back, as well as the curve of her ass, and then down the back of her thighs. Diana was mewing, noises of joy and contentment that I broke by tightly pressing my hand against her right side, a sharp cracking sound that took her off balance.

"Oh, no! That hurt, sir!" She screamed, but she didn't try to flee. I was certain that I had not struck her too strongly.

"Don't complain, otherwise things would be much harder for you," I warned her.

Diana whimpered as she wiggled around on my knee, "Yes, sir." She gasped out again but didn't protest after another somewhat rough slap on her left eye. Her cheeks were both peach and seemed attractive. I repeated my pattern, slapping each cheek twice more, and Diana's moisture oozed onto my leg. "Please, Sir, I've had plenty. I'm going to be a nice kid. I guarantee it!"

"It's not looking positive right now. It's okay to be a bit naughty."

"Sir, indeed! I'll prove to you how naughty I'm always capable of being!" Diana sprang on her feet, took off her top, rolled me onto my back, and assisted me in swinging my legs until I was on my bed in the right direction.

Still, I couldn't say her because my mouth was preoccupied with kissing her lips and then her clit. Her reddish cheeks shimmied just in front of my eyes as I pounced on her most delicate spots, which I had memorized by that time. She was still worked up, so I got a little trickle of her delicious juices that saturated my cheeks and jaw.

Diana said with a wicked grin, "Who is being mischievous this time? I will have to spank you the next time we get together.

Just not right now. I'm way too hot for you." She got down to her knees and knelt, her head resting on a cushion.

"You're a bad kid," I exclaimed with mind-numbing delight. "And I wouldn't alter a thing about you for the universe. Keep being naughty for me!"

Diana exclaimed, "My pleasure, boy." "You must be my evil, sexy guy."

We finally calmed down, and after exchanging more kisses, I realized the time was nearly 3:30. I informed Diana we had to get washed up and downstairs by 4, so we dashed to my bathroom and took a short shower. Ten minutes in the bathroom, ten minutes drying and grooming (Diana used a shower cap to keep her hair dry), and ten minutes getting ready and straightening out my bunk. To freshen the weather, I sprinkled some space freshener around. When we dressed appropriately, we went downstairs to get something to drink before putting on some music as though it were some other day.

Cammy returned home some 15 minutes later, overjoyed to see Diana. Cammy embraced both of us and told us about her friend's birthday party. Then she went upstairs to transform into more comfortable clothing, and my parents arrived when she was out. Diana and I assisted them with the bags, and mom welcomed her to dinner.

That night, we brought Cammy to play mini-golf and then ice cream. We became the epitome of a young couple in love. Cammy didn't even look at Diana and me as we kissed. She was thrilled to see us in that state.

I went to Diana's the next day for a while, and we spoke once more until she signed her contract and mailed it. She was finally leaving for the summer. We'd be apart for most of July and August. We were hoping that as a couple, we'd be confident enough to pull it together. Just time will say.

Diana and I didn't have as much 'fun' time together as we would have wanted or as much as we were accustomed to during the next four weeks. Exams had to be taken, and final articles had to be published. We entered an informal discussion group of around 15 people who met a couple of afternoons a week to exchange ideas and generally support each other. Back then (and still today), New York State was the only state requiring Regents exams in various topics. You didn't have to take any subject. Still, you had to take English and Social Studies, a foreign language, and a three-course category of science or math (algebra, geometry, trigonometry, or genetics, chemistry, physics, and earth science) with a specific form of degree. I'm not sure why this was important. But it was true. The best thing was that Diana developed some friendly contacts even though it was late in the year.

Diana has previously completed both of her Regents and took all AP courses and graduate-level classes to gain college credits. I was taking two AP courses, English and History, when she was taking five. Overall, my girl was brilliant. So, with all of the learning and my internship, we just had Friday nights to have fun. Often it was just a bite to eat and a movie; on other occasions, it was a function to attend, and we always had time to indulge our sexual lives, but not as much as we had been used to.

Seniors' exams were finally completed on Friday, June 15th. The 19th was the date set for graduation. The Friday night was a big gathering, not entirely legal, but everyone who wanted to participate chipped in to get four kegs, which we schlepped to an NYC public park, off the parking lot, where there was a lot of drinking and music. Several joints were moved about. I restricted myself to two beers....well, two and a half....because I was driving, but Diana went a bit crazy, something she rarely did before and got pretty wasted. She wasn't inebriated, but she was fairly buzzed by midnight.

Diana wrapped her arms around my neck and replied, more loudly than she usually did in public, "Hello there, sweetheart. If you want to take me anywhere and take me hard?"

A few people nearby laughed loudly as they saw her. This was a version of Diana that no one in our class has ever seen. It was just a matter of time before word got out.

"You seem to be a little blasted, honey. I believe we can go get you some coffee before I drive you home." I didn't want to exploit her partner or not. Besides, Diana wasn't looking her best at the time.

"Honey, I guess we should wake you up a bit. After that, we'll be able to work out the lot. Come on, my darling." I pulled her to my vehicle, sat her in her seat, and fastened her seatbelt. I got in my car and drove to yet another diner (there were dozens of them throughout Queens back then, all owned by Greek-Americans, like it was a law or something). Diana noticed where we were as I pulled into the parking lot and said in a moaning voice I'd never heard from her before, "Hello there! I assumed we were going to get married!" I couldn't stop myself from laughing uncontrollably. It was way too amusing. "What are you laughing about?" she mumbled. It took some time for me to recover from my laughter. Diana didn't get what was so amusing. "What are you laughing at, Jon?" she inquired.

"Please accept my apologies. You're only really amusing right now. Let's go inside for a coffee and toast." When we got there, I made sure she had two cups of coffee and a toasted bagel. I drank tea and ate a bagel. We didn't say much; we took our time and let time and coffee do the talking. Diana was sobering up for only an hour and a half, but she wasn't doing much healthier. "I can't believe I got so drunk," she admitted, her face paler than normal. "It's like death has frozen over."

"I've been there a couple of times. I'm not a major drinker, which could come in handy when we get to work. Smoking marijuana, on the other hand...safer, that's in my opinion. You don't feel ill from it, nor do you get a sickening hangover from it."

"Yeah, I'm sure it's fantastic, but it's illegal. If you are caught, your life could be tainted by a criminal record. It should not be unconstitutional, in my opinion; however, it is. Anyway, thanks for looking after me and not using me for love, sweetheart. I'd have hated it as I sobered up, so I thank you for not taking advantage of my drunkenness."

"You weren't in a situation to make an informed choice, honey. I respect you so much to hurt you like that. In the next two weeks, we'll have plenty of time for intimacy. Following that...."

"No, not too many. My next cycle isn't expected until the first week of July, at the very least. I'd like to see you as soon as possible before I go. Just not tonight, "She said, weakly nodding.

"You've struck a bargain. Are you happy to go home, in your opinion? Can you believe you're sober enough?"

"Jon, you are right. Please get me home. And once more, thank you. Another excuse to adore you." She held my hand in hers. I charged the bill, and we got in the car to drive around.

Diana said when we arrived at her house, "You don't mind if I don't want to make love to you tonight? I despise saying no to you."

"Diana, please don't ever sound as though I'm putting pressure on you. And let me know if you feel it. There will still be other nights and days. I'm excellent. It's fine if you can't kiss me goodnight. I realize you're feeling under the weather."

17

"More than a bit," she attempted to grin. "I suppose it's not that horrible. I don't believe I'll get ill. Jon, thank you for being so kind to me. I adore you to the moon and beyond." She reached in and embraced me tightly. Except for a quick peck, there were no kisses.

"You get your shut-eye, honey. You're focusing on your speech for tomorrow, aren't you?"

"True. Salutatorian is a salutatorian. It's a big deal."

"Hey, it's kind of a huge deal. That day in the hall, when I first saw how lovely you are, I told you that so many of us wish we had your intelligence and would love to be delivering that speech. You should be pleased with yourself. Your families will be pleased with you. Except for Will and Walt." That made us all laugh; they'd be very proud of their sister. "Don't forget that I'll be proud of you," I promise my heart would burst with pride. Not to mention my parents and Camilla. "In particular, Cammy."

Diana gripped me ever more tightly. "I wish I didn't have to quit you or that I could welcome you in for the night." "I'd like to wear you all night."

"I wish we could as well." Tomorrow night, we'll head back.""

"Or we might hang at home." My parents are heading out tomorrow night, and Will and Walt will almost definitely head out for a few hours. Please contact me in the afternoon of tomorrow. "I adore you, Jon."

"I adore you, Diana." "Thank you very much."

We kissed goodnight, and I led her to the entrance, making sure she wasn't wobbly. I went home, missing her after she went inside. I snuck out a pair of panties she had sent me before going to bed and jerked off furiously, thinking about my sweet, gorgeous, and brilliant queen. Cumming wasn't quite as enjoyable as Diana's, but it was everything I had that night. Thinking of her was such a big turn-on. I hid her underwear once more before turning over and falling asleep.

XXXXXXXXXXXXXXXXXXXXXXXXXXXXXXXXXXXXXXXXXX
XXXXXXXXXXXXXXXXXXXXXXXXXXXXXXXXXXXXXXXXXX
XXXXXXXXXXXXXXXXXXXX

After I got home from work (tired as hell!) and before I went to bed for a two-hour sleep, we spoke after I got home from work. It was necessary if I was to spend the evening with Diana without falling asleep on her. With a literal sense. I may have dozed off as we were making love; that's how tired I was. I awoke at 6:30 a.m., showered, dressed, and spent some time with my dad.

"What are your plans for tonight?" Cammy inquired, the brightest, brattiest grin on her face. I believe she was hoping to accompany us if we headed out anywhere.

"I'm sorry, Kiddo, but we're all hanging out tonight," I swear we'll take you out one night before Diana leaves for the summer. And you'll see her at the graduation ceremony on Tuesday." They were eating, and I was starving, so Diana and I took Chinese food for dinner. Mom's potted chicken, on the other hand, smelled delicious.....

"In truth," my mother chimed in, "would you mind watching your sister next Saturday?" We're going to spend the day at Sandy and Marvin's house. You wouldn't be willing to accompany us?" She sent me a similar glance.

"I don't see how Mom." The only explanation I'd go will be if Adrienne is there because we're not talking right now. We may be finished as partners."

"What happened between you and Adrienne, Jon?" Camilla inquired. My father was aware of the problem, and I thought he informed my mother, but Cammy...well, I couldn't describe it to a 12-year-old.

"I'm sorry, Cammy, but it's not anything I can discuss with you. It's more appropriate for adults."

"Does it have anything to do with sex?" My precocious sister blurted out, and I was relieved that I wasn't feeding or I might have swallowed on something. I shouldn't have been surprised; my sister was almost as smart as Diana. She was also very wise.

"Camilla Rose!" my mother exclaimed emphatically. "It is not a question you should be asking your buddy!" His personal life is his own, and besides, if you want to know something about sex, just ask me! And then I'll know whether or not to inform you!"

Cammy seemed to be angry. She didn't do something bad at all. She was getting closer to maturity, and she was intrigued. However, some things became much too intimate, particularly between an older brother and his younger sister. "Cammy, Adrienne, and I fought," I said softly. The reasons are really specific, but it was a poor battle, and I'm not sure whether we can mend things between us. I'm hoping we will because I'm missing her. I suppose only time can tell. Still, I can't tell you much about it."

Cammy seemed to recognize it, even though she wasn't thrilled with it. I assured my parents that I would take care of her. Diana and I will spend the day doing things with her. It was then time for me to head to Diana's.

Camilla approached me as I approached my front entrance, just as I was about to leave. "Who is Jon?" I apologize if I asked you a question that I shouldn't have. "I have no idea."

I knelt to eye level, which needed less and less bending all the time. She was getting higher and higher every day. "No, you have no idea. But there's plenty to be sorry for. I'll gladly answer most of your questions. That's why you have a big brother. But there are certain topics I just cannot discuss. Maybe when we're older. MUCH older. "Like when we're in our sixties." She burst out laughing and embraced me.

"Hi, Diana!" she screamed as she dashed up the stairs to her place.

"I'll do it!" I chased her down and went to Diana's. Five minutes later, I was kissed on the mouth by my best lips in the whole universe. In full view of her relatives. She was making up for the night before when I didn't get a goodnight kiss.

22

"Hello, sweetheart," Diana said quietly, kissing her gently. "Do you miss me?"

"Throughout the day. "Seeing you helps relieve the agony," I said, smiling.

We went to her family's living room and stayed for ten or fifteen minutes, often talking to her parents, before the twins left for a friend's house after their father ordered them to be home by ten o'clock. Diana informed me that she had already arranged for dinner and that it will be delivered shortly. The benefit of having a partner who understands you too well is that she knows what to order for dinner without having to think.

Dinner arrived ten minutes later, and her parents left a few minutes later. We were alone, enjoying dinner and looking forward to more alone time. "How did you sleep the night before?" I inquired as we ate a chicken and shrimp dish with potatoes.

"I fell asleep as soon as I placed my head on the couch, but I was up at 6 a.m., peeing and feeling nauseated." I got some water and drank it slowly, and by 7 p.m., I felt much stronger. Then I slept until ten o'clock and felt good."

"You're fortunate. Any citizens may have been sick the whole day. Except for graduation, you should feel relieved that school is done. "You made a bit of a scene last night," I said with a wide grin.

"How come?" "What did I say or do?" Diana inquired, alarmed.

"You mentioned bringing you somewhere and taking you roughly. It's very loud. I'm talking about LOUD. Then I said that we wanted to get some coffee.

Diana came to a halt in the midst of swallowing whatever was in her mouth. She became as white as a wall. "No, I didn't."

"All right, you didn't. And that you did. "I swear to God."

"Oh my goodness! I'm not going to the graduation ceremony on Tuesday! I'm not going to expose my face in front of those strangers!"

"Of course you will. It would humanize you in the eyes of all who believe you're some kind of arrogant genius. "You, like the majority of us, are a human being." I was on the brink of laughter when I smiled.

"I'm happy you find this amusing. "How come you didn't stop me?"

"I couldn't put an end to you. I have no clue what you were trying to suggest because you were shattered. After that, I got you out of there. Still, people saw you. Don't worry about it. You'll joke with them about it at our tenth anniversary."

Diana didn't understand the joke. She was doing a gradual burn when she threw away the paper plates and put the leftovers in the fridge. I approached her from behind, wrapping my arms around her tummy and kissing the side of her cheek. Diana tried to resist me at first, but when I kissed her cheek to the side of her mouth, then the back of her neck and shoulders, Diana's icy cold attitude melted away, and she soon turned to face me, returning my kisses with all her desire. Her arms were wrapped around my waist, and her lips were kissing mine. Then she kissed the side of my neck and the back of my throat, and I was listening to her advances.

"You remember, sweetheart, I never got to be my king's serving wench. Why don't you take me upstairs, my King, and do whatever you want with me? "I can be accommodating."

"Affordable? "Let's see how accommodating you are," I said as I picked her up and lifted her the stairs to her bedroom over my back. Diana burst out laughing as she bounced along with my steps.

"It's Jon!" "Please, put me down!" She burst out laughing, her earlier anger forgotten. "I've just eaten!" "You're going to make me puke all over your ass!"

"Then you'd best not vomit!" Vomiting on the King is a capital offense!" I threw her on her bunk, and she burst out laughing like she was Cammy's age.

"Sire, did I offend you in some way?" "Did I say anything to irritate you?"

"Not at all, my wench. We've already agreed we have to have you. And have you we shall," I said commandingly as I began removing my top and undoing my trousers. "So, baby, what are you waiting for?" "Take off your clothes for your King!"

I screamed like I pretended to be rain.

"Indeed, my King. And accept my apologies for the wait." Diana hurriedly changed out of her clothing. Her skin tone was pinkish, and her desire was visible all over her body. My curiosity was visible through my body when my shorts were off. The head was reddish, on the verge of turning black. Diana licked her lips unintentionally.

"Please come here, child, and serve your King." "Don't you know what to do?"

"I think so, my Lord." If not, I'll find something out." Diana was on all fours in front of me, her mouth moist and needed, while I stood by the side of her bunk.

"Yes, my wench, that is fantastic. "Just wonderful," I said, again and again, urging Diana to use her oratory skills to bring me great joy. She moved back to my balls but not using her fingertips. As I looked along her back, I noticed the great curves of her hips narrowing until flaring high from the width of her fantastic butt. I kept asking how I had overlooked her sexiness and elegance all those years.

I could scent her, sweet, beautiful, feminine, filling the space, yet as horny as she must have been, she stayed in character, completely submissive. Yet I couldn't make her that helpless. She stared up at me, puzzled. "Did I offend you, my King?"
"No way, my poor daughter. I just want to try you out as well."
We both laughed; the vocabulary was, to put it mildly, florid. But it was entertaining and a little kinky, and we were having a good

time playing the game. "Stay just where you are; don't shift." Then I broke character and kissed her many times, receiving a huge smile in exchange.

I stepped behind her and climbed into the bunk, placing my palms on her cheeks and softly and lovingly touching her while I began to lick her butt all over. Maybe a true king might not have bothered to be so loving, but I wasn't a true king. "That feels so wonderful, my King," Diana said with a long, deep sigh. "You might claim it at any moment."

Diana moaned and shuddered as I took my first bite, and when I licked and kissed her gash and lips more vigorously, her lower body rolled about a little more wildly, and the groans I heard drove me to devour her delicious slit.

"My lovely lady. You're incredibly tight. "I sighed. "You're fantastic."

"Thank you so much, King. You're in a great mood." I began thrusting, gently at first, bending over her and kissing the back of her neck, causing Diana to shiver all over. She giggled a lustful laugh that fueled my need for her even further. We spoke less as I went quicker, so we could just appreciate our sexual gratification. I had a layer of sweat on my neck, and the smell was blending with Diana's feminine scent. "Harder yet, my King," she grumbled. "Please fuck me some more!"

"As you wish, my love," I said, quickening my pace. It was a beautiful experience any moment Diana and I was together, whether we were acting like two depraved sex maniacs or being as caring and tender as possible. This time, it was unmistakably the former. Wicked, filthy, and a lot of fun. I offered her a light spanking, and she yelped gleefully from the surprise and sting.

My climax did not sneak up on me; rather, it erupted from inside me. My balls drew tighter to my body and twitched like Diana, and I let go of my seed inside her. My hips continued to pump, churning our milk into foam. Diana slid forward softly, and I drifted with her, nestling her smooth butt into my lap. We were exhaling heavily when Diana said quietly, "Thank you so much, my sexy King. You're too kind ", and we all laughed. Diana stretched catlike before reaching back over her head to caress the back of my neck and arm, and I nuzzled her neck and shoulder.

Brow. My hands sought her breasts and curves, and she sighed as I moaned as she sighed.

"You're too much fun," I said next to her ear, causing her to turn her head back towards me. "It's even sexy."

"You're just a lot of fun, sweetheart. And you are welcome to be my King at any time. "Diana said this as she turned to kiss my lips. "Pretty much at any moment."

When I remembered to remind her, we cuddled for a bit. "I almost forgot about it. I informed my parents that Camilla would be taken care of the next Saturday. They'll be out all day and into the evening."

"Not a challenge. We'll find something enjoyable to do. Just bear in mind that this is our last weekend together until I go. Staff must be present the next Thursday for four days of orientation, even though they have already served there. But this is our last Saturday night together for the next two months." Diana will be away for more than eight weeks; it was beginning to set in. If our schedules aligned, I'd see her once a week. I squeezed her as much as I could without harming her.

I changed the topic and asked, "What else is there to say? Our families will gather at graduation on Tuesday."

"You know, I didn't even consider it. Is there anything to be concerned about?"

"I can't believe so," I replied. "Maybe we should all head out to lunch after that. I'll tell my parents about it tomorrow."

"I'll do the same thing. Why am I concerned about the prospect? "She inquired of me.

"I'm not sure. I'm in the same boat, so there shouldn't be any problems." Even the concept was strange.

We woke up, washed up, and then straightened her room before getting ready before her brothers arrived home. She took the notes for her Salutatorian speech downstairs and read them to me, asking for feedback on some points, wording, and principles. I sent her some suggestions, some of which she approved and some of which she refused. It didn't bother me; it was her voice, and it had to sound and feel right to her. Will and Walt arrived home about 20 minutes late, just when Diana began to worry, but she vowed not to warn her parents about their tardiness. They sat with us, and by that time, they had warmed up to me. They weren't as close to me as Cammy was to Diana, but we got along well.

We went out to find something to drink when her parents got in. After the night before, it was strictly something soft, but we went to another tiny local club with live music and danced for a couple of hours, some quick hits but more when things slowed down, in between enjoying a couple of club sodas. We shuffled on the tile, Diana's head turned sideways on my chest, her head coming straight to my lips for an easy kiss. It was fine after our previous activity and enjoying each other.

I brought her home at 2:30 and went home after several kisses— Goodnight at her entrance. We took Walt, Will, and Camilla to the Mets game the next day. We sat way up in the $1.50 cheap seats (1979, remember?) and had a wonderful time, with my parents paying for hot dogs and Cokes. Cammy, who isn't a major baseball enthusiast, was well-behaved and got along with Diana's brothers. It was just an enjoyable afternoon that seemed completely normal. When I dropped Diana and the boys off at home, we asked her parents if we should have lunch with my dad, and they agreed it seemed like a nice idea. When I got home, my parents liked the concept and said it was time to meet her relatives.

On Monday, we each did our own thing; I played softball with colleagues, and then a group of us got haircuts (every barber and hair salon was packed that day!) Diana and her mother went shopping for camp uniforms. At 10 a.m. on Tuesday, we graduated from Queens College's auditorium. I got up, showered, washed, and dressed up in my finest suit and tie. Since I was anxious, I missed breakfast and instead drank some juice. My family was all dressed up, including Cammy, who was wearing a bikini. She stood next to me in the living room as we waited for our parents and said, "I'm so proud of you, Jon," and gave me a huge hug. I was taken aback and shed a little tear when I embraced her back.

"Thank you, Cammy. You that I'm proud of you as well. I'm grateful you're my niece. And though you might be a jerk at times." She giggled when I looked down at her. So to say, the other lady of my world.

We left early enough for me to stop at the florist to get mom yellow roses to thank her for being my mom, and I got Camilla a single white rose because she was my sister, and I didn't want to miss her out. They were all moved, and my father gave me a pleased look. We arrived at graduation at 9:30 a.m., half an hour early. I drifted about, greeting different friends until coming across Diana and her family. We exchanged soft kisses, me in my red cap and gown and Diana in her white ensemble. We crossed over to where my family was waiting and introduced ourselves. Diana burst into tears when I handed her the dozen red roses I had gotten for her from my father. "Dammit, Jon, now my makeup is going to be a shambles!" In front of our parents and the senior class, she embraced and kissed me. "I am so going to make this up to you tonight!" she said in my ear. Of course, more photographs were made, of Diana and me together, of all of us with our respective families, and we also had someone taking a photo of everybody all together. We felt like a large extended family.

We stood next to each other (we both had "G" last names, Glazer and Grossman) and locked fingers when the ceremony began. Then she was called up to give her address, and I sat there, perhaps almost as proud as her parents, as she gave a fantastic 10-minute speech. As she sat down again with me, I couldn't save myself from embracing her in front of everybody, and we were greeted with cheers and catcalls. After Elizabeth finished her address, we took turns receiving our diplomas by the last name, and everybody flipped their tassels to indicate that we were finally graduates. The students exchanged handshakes and cheek kisses. It was almost done. The next chapter in our lives was about to start.

Our parents got along well at lunch, which was at a busy Italian restaurant where my parents had invited them all over for a little barbeque on Sunday. That night, though, there was a huge party at a nearby bar that the class had rented out with a DJ, and it was a lot of fun. Diana and I stayed mostly sober (neither of us wanted to replay the previous week), but it didn't stop us from having a wonderful time, chatting and joking with friends, and dancing the night away.

My friend Mike came over, a little tipsy, and said, "I'm delighted for you! You two make such a cute pair!" He was slurring his thoughts, and I was relieved that he lived two blocks away and could walk alone. We laughed when we thanked him, but I was concerned about the people who drove there and the amount of alcohol we consumed. Diana and I discussed it, and we gathered about a half-dozen sober people to volunteer as a driving service for our classmates who were too intoxicated to drive. Starting at 1 a.m., we took turns filling up our vehicles for everyone that wanted a lift, driving them around, and then returning. It took two to three drives for each of us to drive everybody safely, but we managed it, and there were no injuries that night.

It was after 2 p.m. before we finished, and as much as Diana and I decided to 'celebrate' alone, we were still exhausted. The day began 18 hours earlier. Diana turned to me in my car alone and asked, "Sweetheart, would you mind only driving me home now?" "I guess I'm too tired to pump."
We exchanged a grin, and I said, "You took the words straight out of my mouth." We'll think something up tomorrow. Maybe we'll splurge on space and spend some time together."
"I'll take care of it." You've been so kind to me. Those roses were the most beautiful present I've ever had, much better than the neckless my parents gave me for my 18th birthday. My boyfriend sent me my first flowers. "You lavish me with gifts."

"Come on, honey," I say. The flowers were much superior to the neckless. It's lovely." It was a thin gold chain with a Jewish star on it and tiny diamonds at each of the six ends.

"However, the flowers were such a nice treat, and they said too much of where your heart is." You're a great boyfriend and a wonderful guy."

We were huddled in the front seat of my car, in front of her building. Kissing and cuddling We were exhausted, but we wanted some intimate time to kiss and chat. After about ten minutes, I said, "I have to go, honey." Either that or I'm going to sleep here. You're in your room. "Along with YOU."

"As laid-back as my parents are, I don't think they'd go for it, particularly with my brothers at home." So, just go, and drive cautiously home? "Make a promise to me."

"I swear to you. In five minutes, I'll be alone. I'll contact you at noon. Perhaps a bit later. Honey, I adore you. "Thank you for a wonderful day."

"No, thank you so much, my darling. You added a personal touch to this. We'll make up for lost time tomorrow. You should depend on it."

On the way home, I had a little panic. I couldn't hold my eyes open and nearly drove into a parking vehicle, but I jolted awake just in time. That jolted me awake long enough for me to get home and into bed. Diana was the one thing I was lacking. I would have given almost anything to be able to snuggle with her in bed.

XXXXXXXXXXXXXXXXXXXXXXXXXXXXXXXXXXXXXXXXXXX
XXXXXXXXXXXXXXXXXXXXXXXXXXXXXXXXXXXXXXXXXXX
XXXXXX

On Wednesday, I had to go to work. I was still working part-time, but I worked a couple more hours than normal, from 12 to 5. I dashed home, hopped into a hot shower (I sweated profusely in the print shop, particularly during the summer), and was ready to go by 6 a.m. I told my parents that I would be arriving home late. Camilla asked if I could drop her off at her friend Wendy's place, and even though it was a little out of the way, I said yes. And if it was a half-hour detour, I might have done it. Whatever it takes for Cammy.

I dropped her off at her friend's house and arrived at Diana's a little late. She didn't mind; she was the most laid-back lady I'd ever seen. "Hi, sweetheart," she said as she slipped into my embrace in her home's foyer. We were affectionate in public by this time, including with her or my relatives. Everyone thought we were madly in love with each other. And her brothers had avoided making fun of us. "I had forgotten you. And I'm hungry! I purposefully missed lunch so that we could have a large meal. What about cacciatore chicken? "Would this be our first date?" Diana's eyes were filled with hunger, and not just for food.

I returned her smile. "Chicken cacciatore looks delicious. And dinner will be served later?"

"Enjoyed at least twice." Let's get going before I pass out from starvation!"

We spoke and kept hands while we weren't dining at Marco's, where we had our first date (we also had the same table). We had our carafe of house wine. We'd only been a couple, a loving couple, for a little over three months at the time, but we seemed like we'd known each other for years. Technically, we had known each other for years, but we didn't KNOW each other for the majority of the period, and as I reflected on it, I hated every day that had passed. It inspired me to see that we have as bright a future as possible for as long as possible. Diana and I were meant to be together, and I was fairly confident she thought the same way.

After dinner, we returned to the Holiday Inn, where we had slept on prom night. Diana was in my lap, and we kissed a couple of times. "We'll have lots of time together tonight," I said, gently rubbing my nose against hers. "Honey, I want to love you tonight." "I want to have fun with you and make you have fun with me."

"If that's what you want, then that's what I want," she said softly, her heart full of affection for me. It made me shiver, not from cold or fear, but a position of overwhelming affection. As we stood there embracing, we each undressed. We took our tops off first, no hurry. Diana breathed in my mouth, gripping the back of my head with her palms, her fingertips running through my hair, while I massaged her breasts in her bra. Her touch was full of lust, and the more she touched me, the more it piqued my interest.

"Jon, you know what that does to me," Diana said as I nibbled at the side of her mouth. You are making me crazy! "Please help me get out of my bra!" Still, I was moving slowly, teasing her, and she enjoyed it while still feeling annoyed. She grew a little forceful with me when I drew the tip of my finger down the line where her breast met her bra, both breasts. My 5'3" 105lb girlfriend was pushing her 6' 180lb boyfriend back up to the bed before the back of my legs reached the mattress, and I fell backward, with her jumping on top of me. "Jon, I need you tonight and every night if we can figure things out." I don't care if you want me to be as good as chocolate or as filthy as mud. It hurts my heart to think about leaving you next week. So I'd like to spend as much time as possible with you. Sweetheart, I adore you. Over and beyond everything." Diana's eyes welled up with tears, and she collapsed into my side, sobbing uncontrollably.

I stroked her hair and burst into tears as well. She perfectly articulated everything I was doing, my worries, wishes, and everything in between. I wasn't crying as much as she did, but this was a stressful case. We couldn't get a space every night for the next week, so we had to make do with alone time every night, in my car or at either of our houses. Even only sharing intimacy, carrying, touching, and chatting is enough. Our other desires took precedence over sex, but sex was going to be a part of that night. We just needed to get over the current feelings that were gnawing at both of us.

"We'll try our best, honey. Let's take - day as it comes, okay? We've got tonight, as Bob Seger tells. We'll think about tomorrow; he doesn't mention it. Let's only handle - day as it comes."

Diana sniffed out her eyes and simply nodded along with me. We kissed as a romantic couple; then our kisses became hotter and more passionate. It didn't take long until we were lovingly undressing each other and kissing all over our bodies. We were soon down to our shorts, me in black briefs and Diana in a rainbow pair of cotton panties. She knelt over me, her groin only a few centimeters from my face, slowly and sexily rubbing herself. She flicked her nipples with her fingers before allowing her hands to drift down her tummy to the elastic of her pantyhose. Then she slipped only the first few knuckles of her fingertips under the band and grinned down at me, as aroused as she had been before. "I need your assistance, Jon. "You wouldn't refuse me, would you?" she joked.

"I considered it," I joked. "But you're too attractive to pass up." Diana chuckled when I flipped her over on her back and pinned her upper arms to the bed. I'd met a foe I could defeat.

"Mmmmm, someone's feeling frisky," Diana said softly and seductively. "You are free to do whatever you want to me tonight, sweetheart." I am entirely yours. "I'm still completely yours." I bent in and kissed her passionately while clutching her upper arms. She didn't exactly want to flee. "So, major fella, what do you intend to do to me?"

"I hope you're still hungry," I said, a horny smile on my face. I went up to her body, my legs then trapping her arms back, just the thin cotton of my briefs keeping her arms in place. Her eyes were glassy, and she licked her lips on purpose, which was very naughty.

"Take a look at who's spoken. I could taste every single part of you. But then, a bit bit about me."

"I'm delighted." She looked up at me with wet, caring eyes as I pressed my head between her lush lips. I bent over her like a pushup, gently feeding her my nipples in and out as her tongue did incredible stuff to me. As I shifted my legs to loosen her wrists, her hands caught my a$$, spurring me on. Then she spanked me with her right hand, a strong hard blow, making me yelp when she did it again, way more than I have ever spanked her. I didn't mind because it made me so hot, and I fucked her mouth with long strokes.

I was physically and metaphorically swept away by the wicked, beautiful care she offered me. The only drawback was that I realized I'd have to find a way to handle her equally well.

As I regained my breath, I went down her body and kissed her, cum on her face and everything. It got all over us, turning us into a messy, creamy heap.

"You're incredible, my darling, so good, attractive, and naughty all at once." "I'm so in love with you," I said between kisses and body caresses.

"It was an honor, sweetheart. I'm in love with you as well, and I'd do something with you...or to you," she smirked. "I really can't believe you don't get scared when you get your cum in your mouth or on your forehead." "I thought guys despised that."

"I'm not sure about the other guys; it never comes up in discussion," I said, and we all chuckled. It was such a pleasure to laugh with her. I kissed her once more. "Wait a minute, sugar. I'll find a wet towel for us to clean up with. Then I avenge myself."

"Excellent! I can hardly wait! Jon, I'm crazy about you!" When I entered the tiny toilet, she called after me. I took a towel, immersed it in hot water, wrung it as dry as I could, and carried it into the bedroom to rid her face of my semen. Then she took the towel and did the same for me, so both of our faces were washed. We threw the towel to the ground, stood up facing each other, and kissed repeatedly.

"How can I now satisfy my lovely lady?" I inquired, trailing my fingertips over her upper breast.

"That's fantastic. But I want more. You've had me all high and bothered. You should reciprocate. "She expressed her optimism.

"Whatever you want, my darling. I'm here to make you happy."

"That's just what I was hoping you'd think." Diana embraced me quickly before falling to her knees. I could see a little moist patch in the groin, and there was a slight hint of her lovely scent in the breeze. It attracted me to her like honey to a bear. I moved my hands effortlessly around her buttocks before kissing her all over the back of her thighs and her cheeks. Diana frowned and shifted her weight slightly, tempting me to put my face in there. "Jon, you're making me sticky. You're the most wonderful lover!"

"In comparison to whom?" I made fun of her. She smiled and opened her legs wider for me. I took the cue and licked the crotch of her trousers, which were warm and damp from her natural lubrication. My nose was pressed against her snout while I licked harder and harder before Diana whimpered. I may taste her and push my lips to hers, but I couldn't ever suck on her or the pearl of her clit like that. I drew her pantyhose down over her a$$ and left them around the center of her thighs. She could only stretch her legs too far, but that was more than enough for me. Dripping juice and exuding a magnificent fragrance reminiscent of her exclusive perfume, I couldn't get enough of it.

"You're such a sweetheart, baby. I adore how much you adore me. "She spoke quietly, touching her boobs with one hand and supporting her body with the other. She continued to press back

44

into my face, hopping about and fucking my lips. I snatched her long mane in my right hand, pulling her head back and forcing her to push out her tits. Diana appeared after I pressed my thumb against her clit. Her muscles continued to squeeze my fingertips, and her anus winked open and closed.

When Diana had had enough, I let go, slipping my fingers free and kissing her up her neck, sending her one more shiver of gratification. I flipped us on our sides and spooned her, which was one of our favorite things to do anytime we had the room to stretch out. She leaned forward and kissed my chin and cheek. "Jon, sing to me. I like it when you do."

"I'm at a loss about what to sing for you, honey." I wasn't at ease performing in front of everyone, not even Diana.

"I'm looking for something soft and pretty." So, because I couldn't think of anything better, I sang 'Ripple,' one of the Grateful Dead's sweeter tracks. Diana's eyes widened as she was positively shocked. When I was done, she said, "You did an excellent job on that! That's a great album. I had no idea you were a fan of the Grateful Dead."

"I'd think the same thing for you. We're all discovering new stuff about each other." Diana giggled quietly as I kissed her cheek. "Unfortunately, you would be absent. They'll be at Radio City in mid-July."

"I'd see if I could take another day that week. If I had a compelling excuse."

"They'll be there for three nights. I realize they aren't all sold out. I'll bring you tickets tomorrow so you can let them know when you arrive for orientation." It was a fantastic concept, but it reminded us of our impending breakup. "I've only seen them twice. Have you noticed some of them?"

"No, the only concert I've ever attended was Billy Joel's last year. I believe our whole class went to one of those series."

"Except for me. I'm not a fan of his."

"Are you serious? The whole city of New York adores Billy Joel!"

"Except for me, once again. I dislike him."

"Oh, I can't believe it! You realize you're mad, don't you?"

"That's what I've been advised. Do you think it's worthwhile for us to have our first war over this?" I greeted her passionately and sensuously. Diana and I were both able to go.

"No, I'm not interested in fighting. Sweetheart, I want to love you. I adore you as well."

That was an invitation I couldn't refuse. We kissed and touched more passionately, and in only a few minutes, I was good and hard, and Diana was equally prepared. My shoulders crossed mine, and my profile was just a few centimeters from hers. Diana's warm fingertips brushed my cheek, and I kissed and sucked them into my mouth. "My sexy man," she murmured as I pushed tighter, her clit on my pubic bone. She exclaimed, her eyes wide open, as an orgasm swept across her body. As our lips parted, I took deep breaths and said, "Honey, I adore you. My sweet love. Angel, my lovely."

Diana was crying again, except this time they were cries of affection. "Gentle Bear, you are really attractive. So cute and attractive." As a result, our pet names were born, names that lasted a long time. Yes, I'm revealing everything, but Diana became my Angel that night, and I became her Bear, or Gentle Bear when we were alone.

I thrust harder and deeper, taking Diana to another climax, and then we switched places, with her on top of me. She mounted me again slowly, then ground her butt in tight circles on my hips with her hands on my stomach. Soon after, she began to move harder, her lovely butt growing and dropping, though I couldn't see it. But I understood what it felt like to the smallest detail, including a tiny birthmark on her left eye. She was bouncing, riding me to a throbbing orgasm, so it was my turn a minute or two later.

"My Gentle Bear, I adore you. Too much to tell."

"My Angel, I adore you as well. These titles appeal to me. I particularly enjoy being your Bear. Your Serene Bear."

"It is appropriate for you. You're big and cuddly and soft, and you're so gentle." Diana kissed my chest and throat, her body glowing and wet.

"And Angel is perfect for you. You are the greatest thing that has ever happened to me. You're as though you were delivered from heaven to me."

"Jon, you're stupid and mushy right now. Yet I like it. You're such a sweetheart. It's no surprise you were a bad wrestler." We both burst out laughing. The way she mentioned it was adorable.

48

"Are you not tough enough?"

"No way. Yet I adore you just as you are, tender and perfect." We kissed many times more. Again and again. We only had a couple of hours, and whether we made love again or not, we should spend the time enjoying each other. And that is just what we did. We laid in bed together for the next two hours, becoming romantic—touches, smiles, and the like, as well as general chit-chat. We exchanged our secrets, which I won't reveal here, but they were stuff that made us together than we were before. And then, at 12:30 p.m., we made love in the tub, with hot water cascading down our legs. It contributed to the warm feelings we were experiencing, and when we were finished, we clung to each other like coils of thread. It was the ideal way to end our evening.

We dressed silently, climbed into my seat, and I took Diana home. We kissed each other for a long time after we arrived, sometime before 2 p.m. "Angel, I wish we could spend the night together. Every night "I expressed my displeasure at the prospect of returning home to different beds.

"I understand, my Gentle Bear. Every morning, I wish I could wake up next to you. Maybe we'll be able to move together off-campus next year. And though it seems like a long time from now."

"Yes, it is. It seems like an eternity. Let's get this summer over with, honey. I believe we're going a bit nuts."

"I understand. It's insane. Yet I know my heart longs for you all the time."

We kissed her goodbye at her entrance, as we always did, and compelled ourselves to come to a halt and call it a night. As I got home and into bed, I thought, not for the first time, how we would get through the summer apart. Despite the time, sleep took a long time to arrive.

I operated for the next two days (still part-time; Sy and Marilyn agreed to let me resume full-time when Diana left on Thursday). They were decent people.) And I spent that night and every day off with Diana. Most evenings, we had intercourse or mutual love, which was equally rewarding. Just as rewarding, to be sure. Saturday, my parents went to Adrienne's parents' home, and Diana and I brought Camilla to Jones Beach for the day; then, after cleaning and showering at my house, we took her to her favorite burger joint dinner.

Cammy began to feel ill as we were dining. She went to the shower, and Diana checked on her because she had been away for a long time. They'd all been away for a bit, and I was starting to panic when Diana returned.

"How is Cammy doing?" I inquired, apprehensive at the time.

"She'll be perfect," Diana said, a small grin on her face. She lowered her voice and spoke to me in hushed tones. "She received her first period. I offered her a napkin because she was sad and didn't have food. She needed to be quiet for a few moments. I recall how unsettling the first time might be. She was aware of what was going on, and your mother had thoroughly demonstrated it to her. Nonetheless..... Could you please do me a favor? I don't think about it. She's a little embarrassed."

"Without a doubt. I will never make her feel uneasy. My younger sister is maturing. Thank you for being there for her, Angel. I'm not sure what I might have done if it had just been me and her here."

"It isn't a challenge. I'm happy I was able to assist her." Cammy then returned to the table, appearing a little agitated. I simply asked whether she was well, and she simply nodded her head. We got out of there as soon as I could get the check and brought her home to rest. Diana accompanied her to ensure her safety before joining me in the living room.

"She's well. It was only a bit difficult for her. The first time will be a painful experience. She'll be fine. I'll inform your mother when they return home." I kissed her passionately, thankful not just that she was there with me, but she was particularly there for Cammy. My parents arrived home about an hour later, and Diana immediately took my mom aside and informed her. Mom immediately went upstairs to check on my sister while I informed dad. He shook his head and let Mom handle it. He thanked Diana for her assistance, and she simply said that it was not a concern.

Then, when I was alone in the kitchen having drinks for Diana and myself, he told me, "Adrienne was seen by us today. I believe she expected you to be there. When you weren't around, she appeared angry."

"How do I see her, Dad? We argued the last time I saw her, and I haven't heard from her again. She should call me because it was her responsibility. I'm sorry, I miss her, but I'm not going to initiate communication. Aside from that, I have Diana's thoughts to remember. It's not reasonable to her; she's aware of what occurred. I'm not trying to do something that would endanger her. She is the first to arrive."

"I see what you mean. I'm just worried about Adrienne. I've known her since she was three years old. But I'm sorry about this schism between you. So I see what you're doing, Jon. Will you worry about it?"

"Dad, I'll pray about it. That's the most I can manage." I returned to the living room with two glasses of iced tea after he nodded. Mom came down a few minutes later and kissed Diana on the face, repeatedly praising her for assisting Cammy, who was asleep.

"Diana, you're a sweetheart. I can't express how grateful I am. Camilla adores you as well."

"I was just happy to be there to assist. Not that Jon couldn't have supported her, but it was simpler for her to support herself with a woman. And I adore her as well. She reminds me of my younger sibling."

We stayed for another half hour until I drove Diana home; it had been a long day, and the heat can be exhausting. Besides, she was heading to my house with her family for a barbeque on Sunday. Not that I wouldn't have preferred to stay the night with them.

I asked her this as we said our goodnights. "Angel, do you suppose we should spend the whole night together tomorrow or

Tuesday? We haven't been out for a night in a long time." I was staring at her almost imploringly.

"Tomorrow evening. My parents would not scold me. They understand how precious you are to me. I need to spend Tuesday alone with my dad, so we can spend the day together on Wednesday as long as we have dinner with my family. Then we'll be quiet for a couple of hours, but I can't stay out that late, Bear. Thursday, I have to get up early. It's like 6 a.m." As we hugged each other, we were very still. "I can't imagine I'll be gone for eight weeks. Over the past six years, I've looked forward to this every season. Every year at this time, I can't wait to get there. And this year, I'm almost looking forward to it. What am I going to do this summer without you?" Diana was weeping once more, and I was crying along with her. Still, I wanted to be there for her and let her leave with a good outlook.

"What's finished is done, honey. I'm sure you will change your mind and spend the whole summer with me. But since I'll be operating throughout the day, you'll have to pursue another career, one that won't be as enjoyable as working at Surprise Lake. And you'll be miserable as a result. That is not what I desire for you, Angel. We'll miss each other terribly, but it's just the season. We'll run into each other again. I guarantee it. If I may, I'll rearrange my vacation days. Whatever it takes for me to see you. I adore you, Diana. With my whole spirit."

She kissed me softly, gently, and sweetly all over my forehead. "Gentle Bear, my great gentle bear. I adore you with all my bones. This is going to be a challenge. If we last the season....."

"If that's the case, we're truly supposed to be. We'll complete this exam with flying colors. You'll see what I mean. And after the summer is done, keep an eye out. I will shut you up in a room and fuck you all day, every day."

Diana chuckled loudly, which warmed my spirit. "You won't have to bind me. I'll be the one that attacks you!" We kissed a couple more times before I had to go. I had to head to the store in the morning to get supplies for my parents' barbeque. Any of our neighbors and relatives would even attend, making it a kind of casual graduation gathering. Mom had bought 40 hot dogs, sandwiches, and Italian sausage, as well as bread, salads, and condiments. Others brought alcohol, wine, soft beverages, paper products, and sweets—a huge group with many people.

When I got home, my parents were already up, wanting to speak to me even after midnight. Mom said after they shared their appreciation for how Diana and I treated Camilla's case once more, "Jon, you must make an effort to make it right with Adrienne. She was devastated because you didn't join us today. I realize she was the one who started the war, and what she expected was irrational. We're proud of you for sticking to your guns and being loyal to Diana. But Adrienne isn't just our friends' daughter; she's been your acquaintance for years. Because of this, Sandy and Marvin will not be arriving tomorrow. Our closest companions. As a result of the two of you."

That hurt me a lot; it wasn't my mom's intention, but it did. "You can't blame that on me, Mom. I'm going to have to worry about Diana. She is now first in my world, aside from my immediate relatives. We're already worried about her leaving for the summer. I don't want to do something that would aggravate our relationship. She'd actually accept if I sorted it out with Adrienne, but she'd be nervous, and Adrienne, after all, should make the first step. It was not my responsibility." I attempted to take a stand.

Dad then spoke up. "I know it sounds a little sexist, but be a grown-up about it, Jon. If you are able, please take the initiative. We brought you up to be a gentleman. Call Adrienne first thing in the morning to want to make it right with her. We'd like them to arrive the next day. They were just three. Will you please?"

I let out a sigh. I was exhausted and wanted to relax. "I need to speak with Diana first. I won't do that until I know she won't get injured. That is everything you would comprehend."

"It's all right," dad said. "I understand; I would do the same if it were my mother. And we see how special she is, as well as how you feel for each other. Simply call as soon as possible." After that, I kissed Mom good night, and we all went to bed.

The next morning, I checked in with Camilla in the kitchen to make sure she was well. She said that she was, and she apologized for wasting my evening. I stood with her as she ate her bagel and advised her not to be stupid, but she didn't do something silly. Diana and I were also relieved to have been there when it occurred.

She sent me a friendly smile and said, "Diana is one of my favorite people, Jon. I'm thrilled you spotted her."

I returned her smile and informed her I was happy I had found her as well. She hugged me, and I softly kissed her back. I then returned to my space with a bottle of juice. I received two tough phone calls.

Diana was the first. I informed her about my chat with my parents after exchanging our I love yous and making some small talk. "Please don't feel pressed here, honey. Tell me if the prospect of meeting Adrienne later leaves you uneasy. My parents are aware that you are the most valuable person in my life. I promised them I wouldn't do something that might damage you."

"I must confess that I wish I didn't have to care about this. And I sound like I'm carrying the whole weight of the world on my back. I almost wish you had just called her and told me later. Yet I'm relieved you didn't. Call her instead. I can't say I fault her for being drawn to you. "She said it as casually as she could. "Maybe the three of us should find a nice spot and chat for a while. If she means something to you, she means something to me."

"Angel, I adore you. Thank you for your patience. My dear, I'll see you at 2 p.m."

"We will be present. And I adore you, Bear."

The next decision was the most difficult. Adrienne detected the third ring. "Hello, Ade. How are you doing?"

"I've been doing well. Ok, for the most part. I've been feeling bad about how I handled you, Jon. I'm so sorry for how I behaved and for not calling you sooner." Then she began to weep, and I let her go for a few moments. Women have been weeping all over me recently.

I finally informed her, "It's all right, Ade. What's gone is gone. I promise we're well. I apologize for not seeing you yesterday. Do you think you and your parents would be able to come to our barbeque this afternoon? We'd both be delighted to see you. Camilla has been missing you as well."

"If Camilla needs to see me, I'm sure we'd be happy to come. Should we have a conversation with Diana? Is she going to be there?"

"She would, indeed. My parents met her parents at graduation, and they both got along well. So her whole family, including her twin brothers, will be there."

"Oh? Are they adorable?"

"Of course, if you want 15-year-olds." We both chuckled, and it feels wonderful to joke again with her. It seemed like an eternity had passed.

I told my friends, who praised me for assisting them. Cammy and I went to the store to get the meats, bread, and salads. She felt much better every day; a little TLC and some assistance from mom had gone a fair way for her.

We had our main grill, plus dad borrowed a pair of barbecue grills from invited neighbors, and at 1:30, he lit the coals to enable them to get white-hot. I took a short shower, and by the time the guests arrived, we were ready to set the table. Diana and her family arrived shortly after 2 p.m. We hugged each other and embraced warmly, though not enthusiastically. We ordered a pair of drinks, and Adrienne and her parents came about ten minutes later. We kissed on the mouth, and she and Diana followed suit, kissing on the cheek and embracing. That gave me optimism for the future for all of us.

When dad, Marvin, and the other men ran the grills, I sat with Ade and Diana, and we all had a heart-to-heart while we ate. There was no animosity, and we did an excellent job in removing the weather. They could never be good buddies, but they might be polite for as long as Diana and I were a couple. Maybe a century.

I got up, offered my father and his friends a break to relax and rest, and worked at the grills with Walt and Will. We kept the food flowing because they had some expertise from their aunt. Then some other men offered us a reprieve, and so on. When I wasn't preparing, I was hanging out with Diana and Ade, and Cammy joined us because we were all among her favorite people. And because we all adored her, we were delighted to have her around.

As the evening progressed, Ade, Diana, and I were buzzed but not intoxicated. It was enjoyable, and they got along well. When the party ended, I walked Adrienne to her parents' vehicle, giving us a few minutes alone to chat.

"Jon, thank you for calling today. I'm sorry for not contacting you first."

"Ade, forget it. It's the past. We're fine."

She embraced and kissed my face, which I returned. It felt good to have my friend back in my life, particularly because she was getting along with Diana. Things could get a lot worse.

Diana and I walked to her house after Diana and her family had left. It was just a 20-minute stroll in either direction, and it was a pleasant evening out. We moved together, holding hands like 15-year-olds falling in love for the first time. We didn't speak about something significant. It was fantastic.

As we arrived at her place, we stood on the steps together, kissing and laughing. "Bear, do you mind if I tell you something?" she asked.

"Angel, you should tell me something. You are aware of this."

"I'm not fond of Adrienne."

That threw me for a loop. "You two got together fantastically tonight. What's the problem?"

"I couldn't place my finger on it." Diana lowered her gaze to where our fingertips were intertwined. "If you asked her, I'm sure she'd answer the same thing if she were truthful. It's a female issue. I'll never forget how she wanted to seduce you not just when you were engaged to me, but even when you promised her you wouldn't cheat on me, and she never apologized; you had to call her. It's certainly not something I'm going to overlook. I'll never lie to you and say we can't see her. She's your mate, and I trust you. Still, I doubt I'll ever be able to do much other than accept her."

"Wow, I must be as deafeningly deafeningly deafeningly deaf I assumed all was well between you two. She didn't say anything as I led her to her vehicle. Are you certain she feels the same way?"

"Almost entirely. Women's intuition is no laughing matter." Diana said it as a prank, but neither her speech nor her eyes were amused. This was serious business.

"Fuck you. How will I be buddies with her? Angel, you mean something to me."

"We can see her together, and you can even visit her this summer when I'm away, but we'll never be friends in our own right. And accept my apologies, Jon. That's just how I felt."

"If that's the case, I'll have to live with it. "You"...a kiss on her nose..." will always"...a little kiss on her lips..."come first." A big kiss was returned with zeal.

We spoke for about ten minutes before I had to go. We decided to spend the night together the next day, Monday, so I wanted to get home, support my parents with whatever was left to clean, and get some sleep. I had a suspicion I wouldn't get anything the next night.

XXXXXXXXXXXXXXXXXXXXXXXXXXXXXXXXXXXXXXXXXX
XXXXXXXXXXXXXXXXXXXXXXXXXXXXXXXXXXXXXXXXXX
XXXXXXXXXXXXXX

Monday, I worked a few hours. I wanted to, so I took off Tuesday and Wednesday to spend as much time as Diana. Sy and Marilyn were sympathetic to my situation; they had met in high school before marrying at 20. They were also grateful that I kept my promise to work for them full-time over the summer, allowing them to plan holidays for their other workers. They informed me many times that I will be missing when I returned to school at the end of August.

When I got home, I took a long hot shower, shaved carefully, and dressed nicely but casually. Tan slacks, a blue and red white button-down top (fashionable 40 years ago), and shoes that aren't sneakers.

Cammy tested me out as I came downstairs and exclaimed, "Hubbahubba!" before rolling on the sofa. I couldn't help but smile; she was having a good time.

"Squirt, I'll know that sometime. When a boy arrives to pick you up for a date, I'll make him so unhappy that he'll run away weeping."

"Whatevs. I'm going to have a lot of options for boyfriends! "She shook her head, batting her eyes. I couldn't stop laughing along with her. When I left, I knew I'd miss her more than my parents.

I held a tiny bag when I kissed mom by the stove and reminded her that I wouldn't be home until the next day. She nodded, acknowledging, not fully agreeing but still not disapproving. It would have been different if Diana had been just a random person I was seeing. They would never have let me spend the night with Diana, no matter how old I was. But they understood our friendship was strong and caring, and they knew the eight weeks would be difficult for me.

I picked Diana up and, after a few kisses around the corner, we went to dinner at a new Japanese restaurant. Japanese food was not as popular back then as it is now. Few people had some clue what sushi was, let alone fried food. As a result, it was going to be an adventure.

We sat in traditional Japanese fashion, with shoes off, legs under the bench, and sitting on cushions. We were given a short tutorial about using chopsticks, which we did pretty well when consuming pickled vegetables. We glanced at the menu, which had nothing recognizable on it, in a daze. We debated it for a long time before deciding that we weren't adventurous enough to eat raw seafood. We decided on Shabu-Shabu, which is a two-person meal. It was described in the explanation how it is cooked at the table.

We thought that meant a waiter would prepare it for us, but that wasn't the case. They put an electric pot between us to heat water, and then two trays, one of the raw meats and the other of raw vegetables, both thinly cut, arrived, along with bowls of sauces for dipping. Diana and I exchanged wary glances; we were supposed to prepare our meals. We had little idea how to boil beef, how long it might take, or what the sauces were, and the workers spoke no English. To tell it was a fun encounter will be an understatement. It was a nightmare for us, with chewy beef, overcooked vegetables, and foreign sauces.

We finished our meal, I paid the bill, and we were on our way out. We were screaming like insane people as soon as we walked out of the house. "Oh my God, that was incredible!" I tried and failed to maintain a regular expression.

Diana wasn't any different. "Never, ever again! I can never consume Shitsu-Shitsu again!" and we all burst out laughing. "Do you want something to eat, Bear?"

"I'm starving! Let's go to Amore for a delicious pizza!" So we went to Amore and finished our Japanese trip with some nice pizza (nowadays, I can't go two weeks without having sushi or hibachi chicken and shrimp). But it is no longer the case.) We noticed a couple of friends from school having slices and invited them to sit with us as we spoke about our summer plans.

"It was the most luxurious pizza dinner I've ever had," I said in the taxi.

"Yes, thirty dollars for four slices of pizza. What a steal."

"I'm not bothered. Not until I have the opportunity to be with you, my Angel. Every second is priceless."

Diana stared at me with those light blue eyes that make my heart skip a beat. "You're such a nice guy. Gentle Bear, please." Diana, my petite sweet baby, drew me close and kissed me sweetly and lovingly. It was fortunate that we were affectionate individuals; it turned out very well for both of us. "Sweetheart, please take me somewhere where we can be alone. I want to get you out of your clothing and into my body. So many occasions as you possibly can. We may not even be able to sleep tonight."

"Angel, that is enticing. Do you like going anywhere a bit more cheesy than the Holiday Inn?"

"Right now, you should carry me to a closet, and I wouldn't say something." I shivered in her embrace as she kissed my neck with her warm, red lips. I rode as far as I could, though remaining secure to a cheap motel near LaGuardia Airport, which was just ten minutes away. When I pulled up next to Diana's office, she laughed and said, "When you said cheesy, I didn't realize you meant Limburger." We didn't mind as long as it was safe. However, this was a low-cost establishment. I was attempting to survive on a tight budget.

The space was tidy, but it was extremely cheesy. Fake wood paneling on the doors, a tiny dresser and night tables, and a bathroom smaller than a walk-in wardrobe, complete with toilet, bathtub, and sink. It would have been unlikely if we had been on the road. But we were staying for the weekend.

Diana excused herself to the toilet as I sat on the bed waiting. It caused some small squeaking noises when I sat down, so I jumped slightly, and the springs objected. I felt I could have splurged a little more for a nicer bed. Diana emerged from the restroom wearing a slinky off-white negligee and sheer pantyhose. For the time being, I've forgotten about the mattress. "Diana, my Angel....you never fail to steal my breath away."

"I'm hoping for a split second. I'd hate to murder you too quickly after discovering you." She grinned as she approached me and kissed me softly. "Do you need to go to the restroom before I devour you?"

"Yes, just a few moments. Don't leave the house without me!" I kissed her back and walked away with my little purse. I had a little treat in store for her. I went to the restroom for a moment before changing into something fun for her, a pair of black satin boxer shorts. I'd been holding them for the perfect night, and this seemed to be it.

When I returned, Diana was lying back on the bed, saying to herself, "You sure went all out on this bed, didn't you, my Gent...?" She came to a halt when she noticed me in my boxers. "That's incredible. Now it's my turn to be out of breath. Bear, that is sexy. Maybe you don't want to be too gentle this time around?" Diana raised her eyebrows.

"I can be your gentle bear or your ferocious bear. You have the choice of being my Angel or my little Devil. But for the time being, what I want is you, my heart, my true love." I crawled into the noisy bed into Diana's big open arms, and we kissed each other long, lovingly, intensely. Our bodies brushed up against each other, heightening our sexual appetite and hunger. We were kissing and nibbling, also lightly chewing, as our heat increased. We would have melted together if the air conditioner in the room had not fitted.

"Bear, take off my nightgown. Please suck my breasts, "Diana begged. We were aching for each other, but we needed it to continue as long as possible to get as much satisfaction from each other as possible. I pulled the flimsy top piece above her head and sucked instinctively at her left breast.

"Don't wait, boy," she said repeatedly, and I had no intention of stopping.

"You don't either," I said into her ear.

"I'm not going to do that; I'm not going to do that." Her eyes were tightly closed but opened wide, her mouth met mine, and Diana climbed onto my fingertips in her pantyhose. I find myself ejaculating big, creamy strings of semen in my shorts and all over her fragile hand because the fragrance was amazing. It wasn't quite as satisfying as raping each other. However, it came close. We were exhausted for the time being, though not quite enough for the evening.

We were huddled together, sweaty all over, and overjoyed. We kissed each other all over our faces and upper bodies. "That was amazing, my Angel. It's really interesting. My darling, I adore you."

"Oh, my great sexy Bear, I approve. That is all we would repeat. Once more, "With a sweet and sexy joke, she added. And she stumbled sideways into the bunk, which creaked harshly. "I understand you're trying to save space, sweetheart, but I have a feeling this bed won't like what we're about to do to it later."

I shared a joke with her and said, "So be it if we crack it. They do not have a credit card issued by us. Let's give it our everything!" Diana chuckled from my lips and beard from the ticklish sensations when I assaulted her, kissing all over her chest and stomach.

"Stop, you insane beast! You're going to get me to pee!" She couldn't help laughing and swatted my ass in amusement.

I stood up and exclaimed, "It is not what I like in our room! This isn't the kind of place that would give housekeeping in the middle of the night! Go ahead and piss in the bathroom!" She stood up, and I gently spanked her when she passed by, sending me a funny/dirty look as we moved.

Diana gently climbed into bed with me when she returned. We were both terrified that any rash romantic moves would shatter the room. We snuggled together for the time being, both in our very sweaty clothing, which was becoming awkward, so we stripped nude, both for warmth and practicality. We had some pillow chat, mainly Diana telling me about the people she was excited to see and hear campers, some of whom were children when she began and will now be Counselors in Training. Her happiness was so palpable that I realized it was the best decision to ask her to stick to her plans. Missing her would be difficult, but we'd be together all year after the summer. Diana couldn't reclaim the summer if she missed it.

I suppose I let her do most of the talking. She finally said something after a while "What about the bear? Are you on board with me?" Her hand caressed my chest.

"My Angel, of course. I was paying close attention to every expression. I was just hoping that going to camp would be a good idea for you. I wish you could see how your eyes light up as you discuss it. That was everything I couldn't take away from you. If I did, I'd sound like a jerk. I'll miss you, so this is just what you should be doing. I know it in my bones."

Diana sighed, clutching me tightly. "Why do you have to be so soft, Jon? This would be so much better if you weren't such a jerk."

"Yeah, but aren't you happy I'm not a bit of a prick?" I said it with a devilish grin, pulling my mustache like an old-school movie villain.

"You have no idea. You're perfect for me. As if it were a blade in a sheath. "In truth," she said as she moved to straddle my torso, "why don't we use the sword?" I'm not through with you for the night." Diana leaned in to kiss my mouth, then my jaw, and finally my throat.

"That's a fantastic concept, in my opinion. But first," I drew her up to my face, "let me try something tasty other than your kisses." I nibbled gently on her right calf.

"Oh, you naughty lad. I can't refuse this bid, "Diana said as she brushed back her long, straight hair. I kissed her calves, tasting the residue of her juices that had pooled there, then she bent over and hugged the headboard as I kissed her mound with the soft hairs there. Diana mocked protested, "Bear, you're teasing me."

"Don't you like it when I tease you?"

"Don't give up, boy! Don't even think about stopping!" Diana arrived a few minutes later, a surge of desire rushing through her body and mind, and she thrust down hard, once, twice, and on the third occasion, the bed gave way and fell to the floor. We all burst out laughing because we were already only eight inches lower to the surface. "Fuck, I KNEW that bed wasn't going to last the night!" We couldn't get enough of each other's laughter. It was way too amusing.

"We'll have plenty to say our mates on how we're such beasts that we broke a bed while having sex!" Diana landed on top of me, already laughing loudly. If any guy had sat there alone and jerked off, the bed would have most likely broken.

We cuddled through our giggles and kissed tiny kisses, but our giggles never stopped. This was everything we'd consider for the rest of our lives. My eyes widened as this fresh, incredible pleasure coursed through my body. Diana licked her thumb seductively when things got a little dry, also with my cum dripping, then began rubbing again, shifting ways.

I reached for her, wanting to hug and kiss her, but Diana clearly said, "Uh, uh, uh, uh, uh, Get fun. For the time being." I built up a head of steam, almost to a shaking climax, and then she stopped, allowing me to shake with rage and excitement. She sat there innocently laughing at me, then she began again, this time using her skin cream for lubrication, and again, and again, and again, and again, and again, and again, and again, and again, and again, and again, and again, and again, and again, and again, and

Her hands were on my upper arms, my upper body was about a foot away from hers, and I maintained that position as we quietly looked into each other's eyes. I'm not sure how long I remained like that for, maybe a minute or five. I had no idea; we were just swept up in the ecstasy of our passion and desire. I eventually rolled to the left to avoid collapsing on top of her and injuring her. I will never do something that would deliberately or unintentionally damage Diana. Never, ever.

We huddled together, our sweat making the room seem cold. We remained quiet, speaking only through our eyes and kisses.

74

Diana muttered, "You adore kissing me, don't you? Don't worry; I'm not grumbling."

"I'm making amends for the many years we've known each other but never kissed. We're only nine years late, in my opinion."

"Do you want to make up for those nine mistakes tonight? And it is what appeals to me." My Angel embraced me many times, and we laughed together. The sex, the loving, and the sheer enjoyable and amusing circumstances were all leading to this being one of the greatest nights in each of our lives. We were making the most of the night, which may have been our last together for a long time.

We sat in the collapsing bunk, smiling at each other and kissing intermittently. And if it was late, we weren't sleepy. We thought we wanted and take a shower to get rid of the stickiness before heading to bed, so we crammed into the cramped shower stall and got washed despite the low water pressure and cold water. We dried off (barely) with the threadbare towels, and Diana said, "No offense, Bear, but if you carry me back to this dump again, you'll be playing with yourself for a long time." It would have been quite amusing if we hadn't known I'd be playing with myself a lot over the summer. "I'm so sorry, Jon. I didn't give any thought about what I was doing."

"It's all right, Angel. I suppose I earned it. This place is so bad it's amusing, like something out of an Ed Wood film. I could have invested the additional $20 in a better hotel. I reasoned that what we wanted were a bed and a toilet. That's what I get for pretending to be a cheapskate."

Diana walked up behind me, put her towel around her waist, and embraced me from behind. As she laid her head on my shoulder, I squeezed her hands. It was both romantic and moving. Her affection washed through me, and I sobbed quietly about how I had fucked up the night. She forced me to turn back to face her. "Gentle Bear, this has been one of the happiest nights of my life. We've had a couple of laughs to go along with some pretty amazing sex. And if you're really up for it, we're not finished yet. So there will be no more tears. My great little Gentle Bear, I love you more than anything in the universe."

"Angel, I adore you as well. You are my whole universe. My whole being. I'm going to miss you terribly. Let me carry you back to your bed....whatever that is." Diana giggled as I scooped her up in my arms like a groom taking his wife over a threshold. As we arrived at the shabby room, I let her down gently before taking off our towels and letting the joy wash through us once more.

"Bear, take a seat. Allow me to do a wonderful service for you."

"You've always done too much for me."

"Not this evening, not yet. Just relax and have fun. Please allow me." Diana continued to kiss my chest, paying special attention to my nipples, which were not as responsive as hers, but it was always really exciting for me. She worked her way down my torso steadily, teasing me in the vulnerable region between my belly button and pubic hair, causing me to shiver and shake. And sigh uncontrollably.

"You're incredible, my naughty little Devil. You make me sound fantastic. Almost often "slowly engulfing me before she worked the head into her throat "Unnngggghhhh" was the only sound I could create, particularly when she swallowed, an amazing sensation that elevated me to a new level of pleasure. My whole body was trembling, like a quivering ball of jello. That was how good my Angel was at serving me. She kept pushing me back so she could breathe, then back into her throat until I was hers to do whatever she wanted with. I might have been done by now if it hadn't been for my two recent orgasms. I had her off of me until I offered her a huge creamy load and asked, "What can I do to help you, Angel? I'm willing to do whatever you ask. All go."

Diana turned around and kissed me before laying prone on her front on the bunk. "Use your skills to get me steaming hot before you fuck me like this, my sexy Bear. My skin is tingling just thinking about it!"

Whatever she fancied. I kissed her from the back of her neck to the top of her back, then down her spine. My right hand's fingertips ran softly along her lower lips as they were between her spread thighs. She squirmed about, a wide grin on her pretty lips, her eyes closed in a relaxed pose. "Bear, you're doing fantastic. Wonderfully done."

"Thank you very much, Angel. It's both my fun and yours. Maybe even more, "I said this while licking her cheeks.

"That's great. I want you to be a part of me for the rest of my life, "With a gentle chuckle, she said. "I never want to lose you. I'll even take you to camp with me like this. "She chuckled even harder, wiggling her sexy little butt.

"They could shoot you," I grumbled as I kissed her shoulder.

"Oh right, we'll just be together all the time!"

I gave her a soft spanking, and she let me move, and my Angel moaned as I grasped her hips and gently pumped her, feeling the fire rise in both of us. When my groin slapped on her pretty round bottom, I eventually picked up my pace, creating slapping noises with my groin. My thighs pushed hers wider again, and I fucked her deeper and harder, both of us grunting and moaning before she arrived. "Jon, my hottie! Don't cum yet, please! Pull out as soon as possible!"

Diana let me go, and we immediately settled in close to hug and kiss each other. I ran my fingertips through her hair and whispered to her, "My Angel, I adore you. I'm fairly confident I'll love you for the rest of my life."

Diana smiled sweetly as she glanced up at me. "I believe I will always love you, Gentle Bear. Forever and ever. And you're such a wonderful lover. Always my Gentle Bear, except you seem to recognize when I want anything more. I never have to remind you of something. My hottie." She kissed my sternum. "I can't picture any other guy being as in tune with me as he is."

We moved in, took turns using the wardrobe, er, toilet, and returned to the ground bed on the low, making us laugh again. We'd be joking over it if we lived to be 90 and were all together. It had been one of the most enjoyable nights any of us had ever experienced, but it was time to relax. We were looking forward to waking up together.

XXXXXXXXXXXXXXXXXXXXXXXXXXXXXXXXXXXXXXXXXXXXX
XXXXXXXXXXXXXXXXXXXXXXXXXXXXXXXXXXXXXXXXXXXXX
XXXXXXXXXXXXXXXXXXXXXX

We awoke around 9 a.m., and after another trip to the toilet, we lay in bed and thought about nothing significant. It didn't take long for our libidos to take over, and we made love slowly and sweetly. It was the perfect way to round off our overnight together.

We scrambled to get ready in the aftermath, not remembering we had to check out by 11 a.m. or I'd be stuck for a second day. Not in that shambles of a bed. We went out for breakfast on Diana after moving out. I ordered a large stack of pancakes, although she ordered a short stack. When we were done, we had a serious conversation about coffee and tea.

"Will I be able to see you tonight? I remember we decided you'd be with your family tomorrow. We should keep things easy by going to the movies."

"That is perfectly acceptable to me. A movie looks fantastic. Maybe the Alien film that everybody is talking about? I like a strong, scary film."

"Will miracles never end? Sure, if you can have it, I'll take it."
We sipped our beverages in silence for a moment. "Angel, I'm
going to miss you. I can't picture how it would be without you.
We can't speak on the phone at night. How much will you
contact me?"

"Maybe twice a week. Mondays and Thursdays, I will call my
parents and you. Each session will last five minutes. Only
enough time to continue and plan our vacation days." She took a
sip of her coffee. "That's going to irritate me. It's much worse for
you; I'm surrounded by campers and mates every day and night.
I'm feeling crappy about it. I sincerely hope you will be able to
attend next week."

"The same thing happened to me. It's the one thing that'll keep
me sane. If you want to leave me that pair of pants?" With a sad
smile, I said.

"With much joy. That way, I know you'll remember me if
you....you know."

"I wish I didn't have to....you see," I joked.

"At the very least, you have a lot of privacy to....you see."
Masturbation was becoming an amusing euphemism for us. "In
my bunk, I have a different space from the ladies so that you can

hear anything. When I....you see, I have to cram a pillow in my mouth." We were all laughing at this stage. "Seriously, none of us should have to. I wish we could spend every night and every day together whenever we like. Or to simply cuddle whenever we like. Even just to learn about it." Diana was weeping, only tears streaming down her beautiful face, but it bothered me to see her in pain. I took her hand in mine, and our fingers were intertwined.

"Take a look at me, Angel." Her gaze was drawn to mine as she wiped her eyes with the other hand's napkin. "We're going to do it. You're leaving for the summer, so it's not like I won't be able to get there in a reasonable period. We may not see each other every week, but we can. I'll go there next week if I can. When you come home, we'll have more than a week before school starts, and we'll spend as much time as we can together. We'll figure it out." I was just doing that for Diana's sake, so I was starving on the inside. I despised it almost as much as she did. Still, we had no choice but to accept it.

We wrapped our arms around each other's waists as we walked to my vehicle. Diana turned quickly and embraced me tightly as we approached the vehicle. "Thank you so much, Gentle Bear. I realize you're as mad as I am, and you're just trying to make it better for me. It means a lot to me. You're one out of a million."

I kept her in the parking lot, unconcerned with whether or not people stared. Nothing was more important to me than Diana. My mates, or similarly so. It would have been a difficult decision that I was fortunate not to have to make. "How do I deceive you?"

"There is no way. I know your heart as well as you know mine. Yet, I admire your efforts. Jon, I adore you. Bear, my huge, sweet bear."

"My Angel, I adore you as well. To the moon and back."

XXXXXXXXXXXXXXXXXXXXXXXXXXXXXXXXXXXXXXXXXXX
XXXXXXXXXXXXXXXXXXXXXXXXXXXXXXXXXXXXXXXXXXX
XXXXXXXXXXXXXX

I drove Diana home and, after doing some housework and changing the oil in my vehicle, I showered, changed into jeans and a t-shirt, and finally had dinner with my dad. They realized that I hadn't been around much this week. I took Diana to see Alien (Cammy wanted to go, but my parents said no way, no R-rated movies for her yet) and, apart from being terrified, we had a nice time just seeing a video. After that, we went out for ice cream (it was a really hot night) and called it a night. We were also exhausted. We didn't see each other on Tuesday. I had to sleep, and she had some last-minute shopping to do, so she spent the night with her parents and brothers playing a board game and watching a video, something they used to do a lot before I came into her life. I went to hang out with Mike and a couple of people, which I hadn't done in a while but planned to do a lot this summer.

We spent the whole day together on Wednesday. Her brothers were away at a teen day-only sports camp for the summer (Cammy was at the same camp, in their Tweens program), so Diana and I took advantage, having very uninhibited sex in her room. Then she spent the afternoon preparing her suitcases from a list, and I assisted as well as I could. We didn't say anything because it weighed heavily on us. We had dinner with her dad, and he came by my house to say farewell to my family for the season. Cammy was in a bad mood. She and Diana were like mothers, and Diana was depressed as well. They promised to write to each other, and we left to spend some time alone. I wanted to send her home by midnight so she could relax.

We parked in "our place" and had our first kiss in my car. We moved slowly, tenderly, and lovingly. We kissed at least a hundred times. Her breasts rubbed against my sweaty stomach, and her knees rubbed against my thighs and cheeks. We made the most of it, and we didn't know how long it would be until we had another shot. When we did get together, it wasn't spectacular. Instead, it was lovely. It looked fine, and it felt much stronger internally. And so, when it was after 11 p.m. when we realized we had to start getting ready to go home, we all fell apart. We cried in each other's arms for the pain we were both feeling inside.

At 11:30, I said, "We have to get moving, Angel. You're going to need some rest overnight."

"Do you believe I'll be able to sleep tonight, Bear? Perhaps a couple of hours. I'm terrified that I'll miss you. I'm terrified."

"That's not going to happen, honey. I'm not touching or even looking at another girl. I'm afraid not. I'm not going to."
Diana kissed me again, this time strongly. "I understand, Bear. Yet I'm also terrified."
"I understand. I'm terrified as well. I'm afraid of missing you. You'll encounter all those hot men, some of whom have already been in college for a year or two. They may be appealing. I'm aware of it."

"No way, no how. I don't want someone else but you, Jon. Not today, and never before." We disentangled ourselves and dressed to go home, although reluctantly. Diana had assumed she wouldn't see me for at least a week, so I would impress her by showing up at the parking lot where the staff assembled to board buses to the camp. One more short farewell.

85

When we arrived at her home, we stood by her entrance, saying our goodbyes. We couldn't articulate anything other than "I love you."

I didn't want to surprise her. "How about I pick you up, save your father's time, and drive you to the meeting place? We should utter our last goodbyes."

"Are you serious? Look how difficult it was tonight. If you want to look over it again in the morning?"

"I do, indeed. I'd take any moment I might spend with you. I'll pick you up at 7 a.m., and we will have breakfast on the way."

"Okay. Carry it out. Please pick me up. Bear, you know how much I adore you. Much than I imagined was feasible."

"The same thing happened to me. I never imagined I might love anyone as much as I love you. Return to. Please arrive at 7 a.m. Attempt to get some rest." I went home, hurting on the inside, after one more kiss. One last day to see her. It proved to be my savior.

XXXXXXXXXXXXXXXXXXXXXXXXXXXXXXXXXXXXXXXXXXXXXXX
XXXXXXXXXXXXXXXXXXXXXXXXXXXXXXXXXXXXXXXXXXXXXXX
XXXXXXXXXXXXXXXXXXXX

I arrived at her house at 7 a.m., politely knocked, and Diana let me in with a kiss, looking like she got almost the same amount of sleep as I had about 2 hours. She embraced and kissed her parents and brothers as I carried most of her belongings to my vehicle. The important ones. Her parents waived farewell, saying they'd see her on Parents Day, the first weekend of August. We drove to a nearby deli where they delivered what could only be found in a New York deli: two bacon, egg, and cheese sandwiches on hard rolls, often known as Kaiser rolls—served with chocolate. We weren't hungry, so we had to feed. So we ate a little something.

When we arrived at the parking lot, I parked farthest away from the meeting spot, and we said a more subdued farewell. It was still excruciatingly painful. After nearly halving the time, I drove to where the buses were waiting for the workers and assisted in getting her luggage out. Someone helped them into the bus, and our last farewell was emotional, but not in front of her peers. "Please call me on Sunday and let me know when I will see you. I adore you to the moon and beyond."

"I'll call you. I want to do so. Jon, I adore you. My whole core." The horn sounded, and she knew she had to get on the bus. She got on, walked over to a window, and said, "I love you, Bear!!!"

"I adore you as well!!! Get a safe journey!!!" "Diana's got a bookyyyyyyyyyyyyyyyyyyyyyyyyyyyyyyyyyyyyyyyyyyyyyyyyyyyyyyy yyyyyyy I laughed at her plight. They can just bust your balls if they are in love with you. She was out with her parents. It was going to be a nice, hot summer for me. Quite LONG.

I stayed in my seat, watching the buses exit the parking lot and hearing Diana's friends teasing her about our passionate farewell in front of everyone. Later, I discovered that her lifetime friends were a mix of thrilled and a little jealous because she was clearly in love. It was all in good fun, and Diana told them our tale on the way up (just the high points, leaving out very personal things...I think).

I tried to exit the parking lot after the buses had gone, but I couldn't get out right away. I had to pull over because I was weeping and missing her. It took me a few moments to regain my equilibrium. I didn't mind if someone saw me. The effect of not having Diana for the majority of the summer was devastating, and it struck me like a ton of bricks.

I had a half-hour until college, so I went early. Cammy was the only one there, and I held her tightly. She understood what was killing me because she was my loving and adoring little sister, and she only kissed me as I had done with her countless times over the years.

"I'm sorry, Jon; I know you'll miss Diana; I'll miss her as well, but it won't be the same. But you'll see her again, and then you'll be back together. Meanwhile, you have me to adore. Jon, I've lost my me and your, period." She backed up far enough to throw me a wide grin. Damn, she was maturing into a woman rather than a boy, in her heart rather than in her physical growth. To let you know, we're all very good friends and siblings after more than 40 years. That's how it's always been.

"Thank you, Cammy. That makes me feel a lot easier. We'll do something at least once a week, or go to a movie or get pizza. It's a Mets puzzle. We will go when the Dodgers come to town next week." She cracked a big smile at that. And I did feel a bit happier after that. It's not anything, but it's anything.

So the summer began. I started working full-time on Thursday, and Sy and Marilyn were as accommodating as they could be in offering me a day off each week to travel upstate to see Diana. Diana sent me the days every Monday night, except the first time I talked to her on Sunday night, the day before camp began.

The first week, she didn't have a day off, which was a total bummer for both of us because we couldn't see each other until the next Tuesday. It was difficult. The positive news was that they allowed her to take two days off two weeks later to see the Grateful Dead concert on Monday and spend the night and all day Tuesday together.

I was up really early on the first day, Tuesday the 10th. The night before, I couldn't relax. I left at 7 a.m., and after facing traffic for most of the route, I arrived at the office before 9 a.m., a little early, and went into the office to wait for her.

I introduced myself to the individual behind the desk and explained why I was there. He shook my hand and said Diana might take me around if I liked. Maybe someday, I thought, and then Diana came in, and it was everything I could do not to sweep her up in my arms and embrace her passionately in front of the four or five people there.

"Hi honey," I managed to say with a shaky voice before embracing her with less than a tenth of my passion for her.

"Hello, sweetheart," she said with a tender yet caring embrace. We embraced hard, not knowing who saw or what gossip could be shared after we left. It felt amazing to have her back in my arms after nearly two weeks away.

"Ahem," Lenny (the man behind the desk) cleared his throat, a grin on his face. I'm sure he'd seen it before; I discovered he was about 40 years old and had been with the camp for nearly 20 years, working his way up to the assistant director.

"We're behaving, Lenny," Diana said, a wide grin on her face. "Did you have breakfast?"

"No, it does not. I needed to arrive as soon as possible."

"Do you mind if I take Jon over to the dining hall and see what they still have left from breakfast?" Diana asked Lenny.

"Diana, you can proceed. At the very least, there's cold cereal, if not something warmer. It was a pleasure to meet you, Jon. Diana, please return here by 9 p.m. tonight."

"I want to do so. Thank you, Lenny." She took my hand and guided me outside behind the office, where we kissed properly in private. We exchanged a big embrace, followed by another and another. "Bear, I can't believe you're here. I've been missing you terribly."

"I understand. I've been keeping track of the days. I'm not sure how long I slept last night, but it wasn't much. My Guardian Angel. I adore you to the moon and beyond!"

"I adore you, my dear Bear." Another pair of kisses. "Let's go find you something to eat. You'll use all of your courage today!" We made a wonderful sound as we chuckled together. We encountered more than a dozen staff members walking with children on the way to the dining hall, and Diana introduced me to everyone, but I couldn't recall their names. It was a lovely atmosphere, with gentle hills and greenery anywhere you looked. The structures were all made of white wood with dark green trim. There was a beach and a large lake (Surprise Lake, right?) with rowboats and canoes. There are a few baseball diamonds, squash courts, and basketball courts, as well as a tiny amphitheater by the lake for concerts and plays. It was picture-perfect. I could see why Diana looked forward to working there every season.

When Diana and I arrived at the dining hall, she asked one of the cooks if he could make me some eggs and turkey bacon. Sure, he replied, just sit down, and he'd carry it out in a couple of minutes. We sat at a table and spoke as waiters set up for lunch in a couple of hours. We couldn't quit laughing and smiling; it was fun just to be together. The cook gave me a tray of scrambled eggs and turkey bacon (most Jewish camps hold

Kosher), as well as four pieces of wheat toast. I was hungry enough to finish the last morsel.

When we were there, her party arrived with her two assistant counselors; all of the girls, like Cammy, were around 12 years old, and they all made a huge deal about me, telling me how wonderful Diana was and how thankful they were to me for allowing her to be their mentor for the summer. She was blushing with humiliation, so I thought it was cute that they wanted to tell me how much fun they were having. And there was nothing phony about it; the girls were fond of her, and I realized I was doing the right thing by inviting her to work there for the summer. She and I might be together for years, if not decades. But Diana was making a change in the lives of those children, and I was so proud of her.

"Thank you very much for helping me feel so at home here. I'm happy Diana is making your summer so enjoyable. It makes me miss her a little bit less. But it would help if you realized that I always miss her. I think she's pretty cool, too." When I ended my meal, we held hands around the bar.

"All right, ladies," Diana said to her campers and assistants. "I'm happy you came by, but it's time for me to go play basketball. I'll see you later tonight. I'll be there before bed search, and you can inform me how much fun you had without me." The girls all came down to the basketball court and offered her a group embrace. Diana took my plate and tray, and we returned to the parking lot and the driveway. She slipped next to me, took my right arm as I drove, and led me to a Cold Spring motel.

"The girls adore you," I said as I followed her instructions. "They have excellent taste." I smiled at her, turning my head for a split second so she could see it.

"They'd have a wonderful time regardless of who their psychologist was. I'm also the one they've allocated to this summer."

"Do you think that, Diana? Is there any psychologist that will be as successful and popular with your girls?" I drove into the motel parking lot and stopped, but we remained inside and talked.

"I'm not sure. I believe so." Diana's vulnerability was showing in her self-assurance.

"Let me tell you a story, honey. I noticed their expressions. I also remember you didn't invite them to visit me. It wasn't even the thought of the secretary. Those girls were eager to participate. They needed me to realize how much they appreciate you and make such a difference in their lives. Don't even presume for a second that you're like every other psychologist to them. They are devoted to you. And I'm sure you do as well. Do not even attempt to refute it. And I can see why you enjoy your work so much. It's a lovely spot to spend the season."

"I adore them. It's enjoyable to play games and sing songs. But I enjoy it when I can assist one of them with a problem, even Cindy or Tamara, my assistants. Nothing compares to that sensation. Thank you, Jon. Maybe I'm a little smarter in books, but you see things about people I don't. And you have a keen eye for me. Better than I perceive myself to be." Diana kissed me and held me for a minute.

I went to get a room, but she stopped me and took care of it. "I insist, sweetheart. Please let me. I'm just so glad you're here!" and she got out before I could object.

Diana came out three minutes later and led me to room 115, which was on the 'down' side and much quieter. Or it will be before we arrived. We used the key to unlock the entrance, and before it closed behind us, our lips were sealed, and our clothes were falling off.

"My Angel, I've been looking forward to this for days. I can't get you out of my head. "Between kisses; I told Diana.

"Every night, when I'm alone in my room, I think of you. I'm doing whatever I can to take my hands off myself while dreaming about you." Our kisses were arriving in quick succession, and our passion was certainly higher than it had been since the beginning of our partnership. We were nude and playing about on the bed in two minutes. We were too hot to go slowly.

We both gasped as the old, yet long-forgotten sensation overtook us. Diana wrapped her arms around my neck and raised her hips to match my thrust. Her legs were wrapped around my a$$, drawing me in and still leaving me there. Her legs and body became tighter than they had been only a few weeks before due to the everyday tasks. Not that I didn't already believe she was amazing. But this was something unique.

We moved in unison, our rhythm so natural and easy to find. I must admit that it was a very fast rhythm. We weren't looking for a leisurely pace here, at least not this time. My hips smacked into hers, echoing around the room. I kissed her tight, time after time, our lips so close to each other that I was surprised they weren't bleeding. Then we hit top speed, and we were seconds away from climaxing together.

"Bear, try much harder if you can! Baby, I want to cum with you!"

"Almost there, Angel! We're almost there..."

attempt to refute it. And I can see why you enjoy your work so much. It's a lovely spot to spend the season."

"I adore them. It's enjoyable to play games and sing songs. But I enjoy it when I can assist one of them with a problem, even Cindy or Tamara, my assistants. Nothing compares to that sensation. Thank you, Jon. Maybe I'm a little smarter in books, but you see things about people I don't. And you have a keen eye for me. Better than I perceive myself to be." Diana kissed me and held me for a minute.

I went to get a room, but she stopped me and took care of it. "I insist, sweetheart. Please let me. I'm just so glad you're here!" and she got out before I could object.

Diana came out three minutes later and led me to room 115, which was on the 'down' side and much quieter. Or it will be before we arrived. We used the key to unlock the entrance, and before it closed behind us, our lips were sealed, and our clothes were falling off.

"My Angel, I've been looking forward to this for days. I can't get you out of my head. "Between kisses; I told Diana.

"Every night, when I'm alone in my room, I think of you. I'm doing whatever I can to take my hands off myself while

95

dreaming about you." Our kisses were arriving in quick succession, and our passion was certainly higher than it had been since the beginning of our partnership. We were nude and playing about on the bed in two minutes. We were too hot to go slowly.

We both gasped as the old, yet long-forgotten sensation overtook us. Diana wrapped her arms around my neck and raised her hips to match my thrust. Her legs were wrapped around my a$$, drawing me in and still leaving me there. Her legs and body became tighter than they had been only a few weeks before due to the everyday tasks. Not that I didn't already believe she was amazing. But this was something unique.

We moved in unison, our rhythm so natural and easy to find. I must admit that it was a very fast rhythm. We weren't looking for a leisurely pace here, at least not this time. My hips smacked into hers, echoing around the room. I kissed her tight, time after time, our lips so close to each other that I was surprised they weren't bleeding. Then we hit top speed, and we were seconds away from climaxing together.

"Bear, try much harder if you can! Baby, I want to cum with you!"

"Almost there, Angel! We're almost there..."

"My sexy friend, Cum! Please put me in now!" She was moaning and coughing, and it was so surreal to see and sound that I had to join her, which I did. My sperm's heat set her off once more. Diana drew me close to her and embraced me as though it were our last kiss ever. Her eyes were welling up with tears, and I was becoming a bit teary too. Our orgasms were fantastic, just what we wanted. I rolled onto my back, pulling Diana with me, and she sat on top of me. If you can believe it, our kisses were much more wonderful than our sex.

We were huddling together as though we wanted to stay safe, but our closeness was due to the need to bond emotionally. Diana's head was on my lap, her fingertips teasing the hairs on my chest, and I could sense her breath rushing through my hairs. I was tickling her spine up and down to just above her smooth cheeks, and I could detect the jasmine and fruit perfume in her fur. We both missed the intimacy more than anything else. "My Angel, I adore you. I can't even try to tell you."

"You are free to experiment as much as you can. My great Gentle Bear, I love it when you say something like that to me. I'm delighted you've arrived. I'm busy all day and evening, but I do have time to think about you. And, later that night... I miss you very much. And I adore you so much that it hurts."

"I know, but to be honest, after meeting your campers today, I'm happy you're doing this. Those ladies adore you. You're having a wonderful time with them. We'll have lots of time together until the summer is through. We'll have the whole year ahead of us, and probably even more. But right now, you're doing something crucial. Those girls need your assistance."

She grinned at me as she sat back on one elbow. "Bear, I'm so fortunate. You're fortunate to be both selfless and compassionate. Knowing how much you love me makes things simpler for me to stay gone. I wish you were here with me all the time, particularly at night, "Diana commented with a twinkle in her eye. "I'd love to make love to you here under the stars. Your passion, on the other hand, makes this split bearable. And the kids are fantastic. I'm having a great time, though I'm exhausted at night. So, what's going on with your parents and Camilla?"

That sparked a discussion regarding our family, and I realized I had a letter from Camilla for Diana. She read it then and then. She refused to tell me what was in it, claiming it was a private matter between her and my sister. I could see it had an impact on her. "Tell Camilla that I'll write her this week; I'll do it after my kids have gone to bed."

We lay in bed talking, catching up on two weeks of mostly minor events, telling her how I was keeping busy, the friends I hung out with, taking Camilla to dinners and a couple of ball games, and quiet nights at home. She told me about her camp experiences and how her closest friends reacted to her serious boyfriend (they were thrilled for her). They probed her with questions, mainly regarding sex, to which she refused to respond. Girls can be very similar to boys in this way. And neither of us revealed anything to our friends. We were mature enough to keep it to ourselves.

Diana said, "You are welcome to join us on Family Day, which is on Sunday, September 29th. Even my family isn't invited; neither is the staff's family, but I asked Lenny if you should come. We'll bring you a t-shirt and invite you to join us for the day's events. Please react positively."

Her eyes begged me to listen to them. I snatched her palms in mine. "Diana, my Guardian Angel. Attempt to hold me at bay. I'll get a bit more fun with you, and I'll be able to see your mates and spend the day outside in the heat. That's a godsend for somebody who's been trapped in a hot printing plant all day." I embraced her, and we kissed carelessly.

"Thank you so much, Bear. Bear, my huge sexy bear." She smeared kisses all over my chest, which I thoroughly enjoyed. I had the most fun being with Diana. She was a fantasy come true for me.

We soon began kissing daily, and one thing led to another. I kissed my way down her body until our arousal had returned. Diana shivered when I touched her most vulnerable regions, which I was well aware of by that point. Her breasts and stomach, for example, were noticeable, but she also enjoyed being kissed at the inner curve of her thigh, just above where her butt started. As I kissed her there, her whole body spasmed, and noisy and sensual noises emanated from deep inside her breast. It was ticklish for her to touch her there, but kissing her there sent her into a whirlwind.

"My lovely Angel. I adore you, darling, and I wish to offer you a great deal of joy. Still only gradually. I'm going to tease you mercilessly!" I said with a wicked grin and sound.

"You're so naughty," she exclaimed, panting. "This is how you tease your adoring girlfriend. If you don't let me cum enough, I may forget you the rest of the day. That is the cock. I'll adore the lot of you." Diana had a dreamy yet needy quality to her voice, trapped between need and peak. I resolved to start offering her everything she so badly desired because I wished the same thing for her. Diana screamed as her body rocked with orgasm as I swirled the tip of my tongue across her clit. The sudden touch had a significant impact on her.

"That was awesome, Jon! More, please? What about me? You're a sweetheart, don't you?"

"Who is who?" I laughed, understanding just what she was joking about.

"The babe who has taught you some new tricks over the last two weeks! Seriously, you sexy Bear, if I didn't know better... I can't believe what you did to me." She kissed me all over my forehead, and I kissed her right back, kiss for kiss. "Every day, Jon, I fall more in love with you. You do the most incredible stuff to me."

"You are an inspiration to me, honey. I only have this incredible need to make you comfortable." She wrapped her arms around me and held me closely.

"Mission achieved!" she exclaimed, smothering me with kisses. "It's now my turn to look after you. I'm just sad I can't reciprocate what you've done for me. It is the fault of biology."
"Whatever you try to do to me, my Angel, I'll gladly agree." I've never had a complaint about how much you support me."
Diana rolled me onto my back and slipped between my thighs. "All right, I'll strive to do something unique for you. Take that as

a matter of honor." Her tongue randomly slithered out and lathered up my glans to a gleaming, glowing crimson. She was off to a fantastic start.

I moaned, often with my eyes firmly shut, often completely open, while I watched my Angel-Devil use her lips and tongue to do the most incredible stuff to my flesh.

"Yeah, yeah, yeah, yeah, yeah, yeah, yeah, yeah My Dirty Bear, you adore it. "And I love all three Bears. Now you're my Gentle Bear, sometimes you're my Sexy Bear, and sometimes you're my very Dirty Bear." "I'm sorry, I'm not a blond," she chuckled.

"I adore you just as you are, Goldilocks."

Diana stood back and kissed my heaving chest and neck, which were sticky and salty with sweat. When I regained my strength, I cradled her in my arms, my little love fitting like we were cut from the same block of marble, our legs entwined, and our bodies melded. We interacted solely by touch; we didn't need to say "I love you" at the time. It just flowed between us.

After some cuddling, we took a shower, dressed, and Diana drove me into Cold Spring. We walked around a little while when we decided to go to a local deli and get some sandwiches and drinks and took it to the town park, spread out my ever-present blanket, and we had a kind of picnic. "Angel, this is ideal. Being around you is ideal. I work hard, but I still get distracted by thoughts of you several times a day. What you're doing, how much more fun you're having, and with whom you have it." I looked down, embarrassed by my vulnerability.

"Bear, you know the last thing you need to be concerned about is me meeting someone else. I'm so in love with you that I don't think of the other guys as anything other than coworkers or friends. Some of them are very good-looking, I admit. But none are nearly in your league, not as far as I'm concerned." She set her sandwich down and leaned against me, hugging me close. She swept my bushy hair away from my brow. "I'm not interested in anything else, Jon." It's not enticing. When I'm feeling sad at night, I still think about you. Nobody else crosses my mind. Jon, I adore you. You are the only one." She kissed me, not a little, cute kiss, but a big, wet kiss, unconcerned with who was passing by or watching us. It was one of the most loving kisses we'd ever shared.

"How did I come across you?" I'm extremely fortunate. "I met my soul friend."

"Because Elizabeth outperformed me for valedictorian. We might not be here today if I hadn't come in first."

"I disapprove. Some stuff, I believe, is predestined. Diana, I believe we were supposed to meet. We would have had to wait a couple more weeks, but we were doomed. At least, that's what I'd like to believe. And, despite how horny I am, I haven't touched myself because you've been gone. But I never consider another lady. You are the only survivor."

"Bear, I wish you'd touch yourself. When you're home in the middle of the night, and consider some naughty, even filthy, fantasies you might have about me. One of them may as well be having fun." She slipped her hand under my t-shirt and hugged my stomach and chest, which was fantastic.

"Would you want me to?" "Jerk off, were you dreaming about me?"

"Who else do I want you to consider?" She questioned, with a 'Duh' look on her face. I grinned, slightly embarrassed.

"That's right. I'll do it in a couple of nights and tell you more about it the next time we meet."

Diana smiled her soft and gentle chuckle, which I adored. We consumed our lunch gently, always touching intimately but not in a manner that might land us in jail (haha). We walked even more after that, arms around each other. We walked into a music shop and looked at the albums, discussing albums we had or wished to buy. I purchased Elvis Costello's Armed Forces and Joni Mitchell's 1971 album Blue for Diana while I had to carry it home with me.

"You weren't required to do that, Bear. I might afford to purchase my albums."

"I understand, my love. I just needed to. It's a fantastic record. That reminds me of something. My roommate notification arrived yesterday. I have to contact him tomorrow. Steve...shit, I can't recall his name right now. He resides in Syosset (Long Island). "We can see whether we'll get together or destroy each other," I joked, "but most importantly, we can organize what we're carrying." I want to bring my stereo; he should bring a TV if that's more convenient for him. You can have mine this week as well."

"I'll contact my parents tomorrow and see if the letter was sent to me." This is terrifying. You can just expect to meet somebody you get along with. I just wish we could have shared a bed." That sounded wonderful to me, so I drew her close. "Bear, take me back to my place." I need to have some fun with you. This time it's nice and slow."

I kissed her on the top of her head, then on her mouth. "Angel, there's nothing I'd ever get. Too long as it's just you and you alone." Diana was gripping my right arm and kissing my shoulder as I drove back to the hotel. We went inside, and instead of removing our clothes, we stood in front of each other and took turns undressing each other. Diana took the lead, gently pulling my top above my head and licking my chest, including my nipples. I moaned quietly, my fingertips stroking through her fine, silky hair. She unbuckled my belt and undid my jeans, slipping them off slowly as she did my top. Diana also assisted me in removing my shoes and socks before removing my briefs.

"You look scrumptious, my sexy Bear." But first and foremost, it's my time." Her voice had the enthusiastic tone that I recognized because I was feeling the same way.

"I can hardly wait to strip you bare, Angel." But I'll do it. "I'm trying to take it about as slowly as you did." I kissed her a few quick loving kisses before steadily bringing her tie-dyed top-up, then tossed her bra aside. I kissed her throat and her body, and she rubbed my shoulders with moans of her own. I knelt in front of her and supported her with her ankle socks and sneakers. And there was her underwear, plain blue, nothing overtly suggestive, but she looked unbelievably sexy in them. Diana was sexy no matter what she wore or didn't wear, in my opinion. To me, it's simply stunning.

I stayed on my knees and kissed her lower tummy. Her skin trembled with enthusiasm, and she clutched my head for support on her feet. Then she ran her fingertips through my sandy hair in a sensual way.

Diana spread her feet about a foot apart so my tongue could sample and taunt her. Her hips swiveled slightly as she giggled, causing me to follow her. But, just when my tongue was about to sample her delicious nectar, Diana softly pulled my head back and whispered, "No, my Bear. I told you I wanted to have sexual relations with you. And lie down for me. Simply settle down."

"I'd do anything for you, Angel." I stood up and kissed her before lying down on the bed on my back. Diana walked steadily as the shadows through the window rose, illuminating her face and body with overlapping stripes of orange and shadow from the blinds. Diana relaxed her body while remaining upright, straddling me on her feet; our palms joined tightly as our bodies rocked softly in sync.

"Jon, I love this," she said, moving her hands casually. "I have a lot of feelings about you. I usually do, but not right now..." As an orgasm flowed through her body, she screamed and gritted her teeth.

"I understand, honey. "I see that as well." My legs were swaying back and forth to rub on her clit to keep her orgasm moving. "I'm madly in love with you, Angel. "I feel like I'll be in love with you forever."

"You're such a nice and romantic person. It's a bit mushy. It's fantastic. I adore you just as you are, my huge Bear. Often he's gentle and friendly, and other times he's hard and manly. "Always the correct one at the right moment."

I began to sit up straight and assisted Diana in adjusting her legs to go straight past my back, then around me, and my legs remained straight. We were sitting up, facing each other, arms and legs outstretched. We were all connected by our genitals and rocked back and forth together. Touching and kissing, sweet and caring. We were able to avoid traveling too far, allowing us to enjoy this fantastic experience for as long as possible. We were almost absolutely together.

Our breathing was slow and steady, and we were starting to feel sweaty again. Suddenly, without notice, Diana's orgasm rose and nearly erupted in her bones, and then the same thing happened to me when my sperm splashed inside her, and we both shook with excitement. We kept kissing, our tongues roaming over each other's mouths, arms, and chests. We stayed seated like that by gripping each other closely.

"Thank you so much, Angel. That was the case... "I can't quite come up with a name for it."

"You'll never need to repay me for expressing my affection with you." But I agree; there are no words to describe how amazing that was. "You are my life's passion."

"How come you have too many other people to equate me to?" With a chuckle and a kiss, I said.

"Hundreds of thousands." Didn't you remember you're just the next in a long line of men I've had feelings for?" Diana said with a huge, sly grin.

We were going rigid like that, and sitting with no lower help was hurting my back. We carefully untangled ourselves before taking turns in the shower. It was almost 6 p.m. by then, and we needed to have another shower together, our third of the day.

"I hope no one smells my shampoo later," Diana joked. "And I believe my skin is raw. I believe it's my vagina. So it doesn't bother me. Just don't let me sprint!"

"Yes, I believe my penis has red spots. But it was well worth it, my dear. I'm already looking forward to seeing you next week."

Diana's amusement had subsided. "Bear, you won't see me next week. I decided to offer up my day to have the two days for the concert the next week. Please accept my apologies, my affection. It was the only choice."

For a moment, I stood, depressed. "If you wanted to, you had to, honey. We'll be taking two days off together. Tuesday night, before I drive you back up here, you should visit our families for an hour or two. We're going to make a deal. Overall, I believe we can come out ahead. Consider how much we'll miss each other by then. We'll make it a memorable evening. I'll book our space at a good hotel in town. It will save you time after the show...and before it as well."

"You have such a beautifully filthy mind, my love," Diana said as she sat across my lap in her underwear. "However, the next time we do this, I'm wearing extra socks!" We had a lot of laughs and kisses together. I'm not sure how many kisses we exchanged that day, but it had to be at least three hundred—even a lot more. We couldn't hold our mouths shut.

We changed into our clothes and signed out. We still had about two hours until Diana returned, so we stopped for dinner at a tiny cafe in town. She couldn't consume wine, but we drank soft drinks with our pasta dinners and tried not to worry about having to split again that night. We only walked after dinner when twilight turned to darkness. The town was quite cool, with various kitsch and vintage shops, various bars and restaurants, and the types of stores that residents wanted daily, such as a bakery and other shops. It was (is) a rather upscale town on the Hudson River's Eastside, a few miles north of West Point on the opposite bank.

We spent our last hour sitting by the water, watching boats and ships move up and down the river, now low dark mountains on the other side, and some houses lit up. It was serene and lovely. We stared into each other's eyes, a combination of excitement and sorrow in our eyes. We didn't say anything because it was difficult to find sentences. We had to get moving after a bit. It stung like hell.

We arrived at the parking lot around 8:30 a.m., with plenty of time until she had to be with her girls. We went into the office, and whoever took over for Lenny at the desk gave Diana permission to carry me into the grounds before 9:30, when they had to start having the kids ready for bed. She led me back to the dining area, where there were several nighttime games with

111

music going on. She introduced me to a few people, including one or two guys who wished they were in my role, but everybody was kind. Diana excused herself for a couple of moments to find her group, and then she took them back to see me again. It was enjoyable conversing with them, and when Diana had to lead me back to the parking lot, a couple of the girls created ooohing and ahhing noises and kissing sounds. Diana smiled brightly, and I waved goodnight to everybody.

A few last kisses in my seat. "Angel, I miss you terribly, so I'm happy you're doing this. Those children adore you. I'm sorry I didn't take your advice; I should have done the same. I'd have less income, but I'd have a fantastic summer."

"Bear, next season. There will already be next year." We kissed one last time, long, short, and sad. She got out of the vehicle, tears streaming down her cheeks, and leaned against my window. "Jon, you drive safely home. Thursday night, I'll contact you. Also, please inform Cammy that I will email her this week. I adore you to the moon and beyond."

I, too, was moved to tears. "I intend to be cautious. I'll talk to you on Thursday. Honey, I already miss you."

"Oh no, now I'm going to sob in front of everybody! You'd best go before I pull you back into my space and bind you up!" She kissed me quickly and hurried forward, so we didn't linger for longer. It was already after 9:30 p.m., and I had a long ride home.

I arrived home in an hour and ten minutes, so I was home until 11 p.m. Cammy was still in bed; her camp bus picked her up at 8 a.m. every morning, she had long, busy days, and she was having a wonderful summer. I went into my parents' space and spoke to them for a bit, offering them the gist of my day without getting into specifics. I was tired at that point, so I said goodnight, did what I needed to do, and fell asleep within minutes of laying down. Yet I was also saddened by the fact that I wouldn't be seeing Diana for the next two weeks.

XXXXXXXXXXXXXXXXXXXXXXXXXXXXXXXXXXXXXXXXXXX
XXXXXXXXXXXXXXXXXXXXXXXXXXXXXXXXXXXXXXXXXXX
XXXXXXXXXXXXXXXXXXXXXXX

The next two weeks were much more difficult than the two weeks before Diana and I met for the first time. I held myself occupied most nights by attending a few Dr. Pepper Music Festival gigs in Central Park, America, one night and The Tubes the next (If you've never seen or heard of the Tubes, look them up on YouTube). They're unfathomable). Five dollars for a ticket was a steal right back then. Cammy and I went to Mets and Yankees games with our father. About how much fun these events were, I missed Diana more than words could express. It wasn't the lack of sex, though we both missed it. It had to be her. All about her is fine. Her company and our closeness.

When Diana had the opportunity, we spoke several times. Cammy sent a letter at the end of the week, which brightened her day (she didn't share with me!). and I received one the same day. It wasn't that much, and she didn't have time for that. However, there was a lot of love in every section, every phrase. It moved my heart and making me feel bad for not writing to her. So, after reading the three pages three times, I sat down at my desk and sent her my post. It was a little longer (I had more time), and it was packed with my passion and heartbreak over losing her.

After seeing Diana, I contacted Steven Lindt, my soon-to-be college roommate, over the weekend. He seemed to be a nice person. We spoke about some general topics and got along; we decided that I would bring my stereo system and he would bring a black and white television, but we weren't going to see it much other than sports and news. Then the topic of females came up. I told him that I had a girlfriend and that we were madly in love. He practically told me that he considered himself a lady's man and expected to be out of our space several times but that he would like to have the room himself now and again. I said that I

114

was certain we should agree. So my outlook seemed to be quite promising.

Diana's case was more complex. Robin, her roommate, came from a tiny town in upstate New York near Lake Placid, not far from the Canadian frontier. And she was a devout Born Again Christian with a vague understanding of what she considered'sin.' Such as alcohol and premarital intercourse. Like in rock music. If she went home on weekends, Robin wouldn't be spending many nights away from her room. However, it was just as far away from Binghamton as Queens, a four-hour drive in either direction. Diana was concerned about just getting along with her.

Finally, Monday, the 23rd, and I were up and out of the house much faster than normal, hoping to avoid any traffic. I arrived at 8:30 a.m., a little early, and this time there was a young woman at the counter, Margie. She had anticipated my arrival, although a little later. She asked if I knew where the dining hall was, and when I said I did, she offered me a guest tag for my shirt (of course, a Grateful Dead shirt!) and informed me I should go there myself. That was another epoch.

When I arrived at the dining hall, I searched the huge space for Diana. She was the first to recognize me and waved from the center of the packed space. I ran up to her, and she stood up and embraced and kissed me like we'd known each other for a year, not two weeks. All erupted in good-natured catcalls and cheers, and I doubt we would have minded anyway. We hugged each other for at least a minute until her party cleared a seat at the table for me. Diana requested a tray of pancakes and turkey sausage from one of the waiters. I was thankful because I was starving and consumed as much as I could. Diana's children laughed as they watched me feed as I'd never seen food before, and she even got me a second serving. I let out a belly laugh, which made the kids and a couple of other counselors laugh. "Girls, stay away; he's all mine!" Diana burst out laughing, and there were more laughs at my expense. It was fine because it was entertaining and humorous.

When I was done, Diana kissed each of her girls and informed them to behave for her assistants and that she'd see them the next night. She was a true mother hen to them, not because it was her work, but because she cared about them. It came from her enormous heart. There was enough room in there for her to enjoy her dad, me, and her campers. It was also another aspect of her that I admired.

We placed her overnight bag in my trunk, got in my car, drove down the road a little, and I pulled over to say hello properly. We hugged and held each other for at least five minutes before saying our I love yous. She looked at my shirt and said, "You're wearing a Dead shirt! We'll need to find one for me before we leave tonight."

"Did you expect to go to the concert without a shirt? Angel, you're a moron." I turned around and pulled a gift bag from the back seat, which I gave to her. Diana squealed with joy as she picked out a Dancing Bears tie-dyed tee in her size and wrapped her arms around me, kissing me all over.

"You're the greatest! I can't believe you went out of your way to help me!"

"I didn't get you a diamond ring, honey. It's just a shirt."

"It's not a shirt!' It's very kind of you to think of it for me. You're a hot, sweet man,"...a kiss on my nose..." Another kiss on my mouth, broad and soft and with a promise of what was to come.

There wasn't much traffic on the lane, so Diana changed her shirt as fast as a rabbit for the one I bought her in less than twenty seconds. Except her top was brand new; she resembled any other concert-going Dead Head. She was absolutely cute.
I returned to the city, and since it was already early (check-in time at the hotel was after 2 p.m.), we returned home. This is my house. Cammy was away at camp, and my parents were at work. I parked across the street, and much as the last time, our clothes

began falling off as soon as we walked in the driveway, but this time the door in question was my bedroom door. We were rolling on top of each other some twenty seconds after we were naked. Our bodies were aroused and wet, and our kisses and touches were improving the situation. We were so in love, but Diana prevented me. "I want to look after you, my sexy Bear."
"You're not obligated to do anything with me, Angel. We're all in this together to make each other proud."

"Don't worry; you'll make amends to me." So I'll go first. You make those long drives to see me by yourself, you buy the seats, and you get me the cool jersey. You've been wonderful to me in a thousand respects.

Finally, I must cum. I could sense her lovely sexual fragrance filling the space, so I knew she was hot. We were standing next to the bunk, and Diana was hunched down, her arms resting on the corner of the mattress. I was beating on her from behind, both of us grunting loudly, both of us on the verge of a smashing orgasm. I drew her upper body back towards me, kissing her neck as she let out small, fast gasps with each thrust. This time it reached me first, and I was spraying her damp tunnel with my sticky cream. Diana sensed it as well, and we all became silent except for our breathing. We weren't doing something illegal, but...who was home so early in the afternoon?

We sat silently on my bunk, only listening before I heard my father's voice...and the voice of a woman who was not my mother. They were laughing together, very sweet, almost intimately. I understood just what it sounded like. I saw it firsthand. My stomach was twisting with a fiery knot. Diana had wide eyes and was looking at me with concern as I glanced at her. She was as upset as I was.

I sprung to my feet and threw on my panties before slipping into my cutoff jean shorts. "What are you doing, Jon?" She hissed as quietly as she possibly could.

"I'm going down there to prevent my father from messing around on my girlfriend, nothing else."

"Jon, love, just worry about this." We could hear them in the living room, their laughter fading into a sexual rhythm we'd seen before. He's a jerk. He's a jerk. "You'll insult the four of us if you confront him now." It's best if you take him off guard and speak to him alone."

"He's about to cheat on my mother, Diana!" I will put a halt to him right now! What if it's their first moment or his first time? I could prevent him from having an affair with my mother! Don't you think it's worthwhile? I may shame us. However, I will save my mother from the most humiliating kind of embarrassment.

Besides, do you suppose we can wait up here in silence for however long it takes to hear them screw? That's what I can't do. "Do you think you can?" She shook her head no, a depressed look on her face. "Please accept my apologies, honey." This is everything I would do. I have to give it a shot."

Diana rolled out of bed, putting on her clothing with a painfully depressing look on her lips. "At the very least, let me accompany you. I will assist you, and maybe it would benefit the woman in any way." Her hand met mine, and we gripped each other tightly. I quickly kissed her and then went to my house.

I didn't open it softly because I needed him to understand me, and he did. I saw him seem like one of the moles in an amusement park's Whack-a-Mole novelty games. Such fuzzy animals were adorable, but there was nothing adorable about my father or the look on his face when he turned to the top of the stairs, where my space was.

"Who is Jon?" "What are you doing at home?" I saw some legs, cool long stockinged legs, running along with the sofa.

"I should have asked you that." "How come you're not at work?" I was already at the top of the stairs, staring down at him, which gave me an edge psychologically. Diana was not the only one who enjoyed reading about psychology. She emerged from my space and took a seat by my side at the railing.

My father worked out what was going on, but he couldn't use that to his benefit because Diana and I weren't doing something illegal, except in a religious way. On the other side, he was unquestionably in error.

"Hello, Diana," he said hesitantly.

"Good day, Mr. Grossman." Her speech was as hard as a stone.

"Hello, Diana. It's Al." "I told you months earlier."

"Indeed, Mr. Grossman." She wasn't going to give an inch.

At that stage, the other lady stood. Without a doubt, she was a beauty, tall with short red hair, a killer physique, and a reasonably sweet smile. I didn't mind. She was assisting him in cheating on my mother.

"I...um...I suppose I should get going." She collected her belongings and slunk down the hall to the bathroom to get ready. That shook me to my heart. The inference was that she had already visited our home. Was it at a gathering? I will have most definitely seen her. Or does it imply that this wasn't the first time he'd done anything like this for her?

I took my time descending the steps. In a shaking fury, I stepped in front of him and yelled, "You son of a bitch."

"I'm still your dad!" That's not how you refer to me!"

"Dad, you always told me that appreciation does not come naturally. It's well deserved. You've lost a lot of confidence today. Don't worry; I'm not going to say, Mom. No, not yet. I couldn't do it to her. Yet I can't look you in the eyes right now. Return to your job. And don't even think about bringing a lady back here to mess around again. I'll mention anything if I figure out you did that. "Believe me."

"What were you doing here, Mr. High and Mighty?" "Are you two holding hands?" My father was angry with me for speaking to him in this manner. Furious didn't even begin to explain how I felt about him at the time.

"I came here with my girlfriend, whom I adore." You can't mean the same thing. In the very least, you could not claim the same." I stormed upstairs with Diana, entered my place, and slammed the door behind me. I couldn't say anything more about him.

We took a seat at the foot of my bunk. I was experiencing a range of negative feelings. Rage, betrayal, deep sadness, and depression would be difficult enough to meet my father, but how could I look at my mother and hide this terrible secret from her? Diana's arm was wrapped around my back, gently stroking my neck and shoulder, but I was so stiff. She drew me back so we could lie on the bunk. I cried as she flipped me around to face her, her fingernails tracing down my cheeks as she looked into my eyes with her lovely blue eyes. I sobbed. There was a flood of tears. I felt as if I were inconsolable. I wrapped my arms around Diana, and she continued to kiss my head, run her fingertips through my hair, and pin my face to her breast behind her shirt. "Let it all hang out, Bear." My gentle and warm devotion. I'm here to help you. I'll be there with you at all times."

Thank goodness she was with me when this occurred. I still don't know if I should have held things intact otherwise. The agony was intense and widespread. But Diana, my true Angel, was offering me the power to endure it, at least for the time being.

"Thank you so much, honey. You seem to be protecting my sanity. In a million years, I would never have thought he could do it. I'm not sure if I'm going to deal with him. How would I possibly deceive my mother? What am I going to do, Diana? We have six weeks before we start training."

"Dear Sweetheart, I'm not sure. I'm afraid I don't have any responses for you."

"Oh my Goodness, Cammy!" I can't tell my mother! It would hinder Diana so that it would destroy Cammy. Aside from her Brother's Little Sister, she is Daddy's girl. She'll be killed once she discovers who her father is..." I jumped up and dashed to the restroom, arriving just in time to vomit the rest of my big meal. Diana didn't sit down, instead of entering the bathroom and stroking her palm up and down my back. When I finished heaving, I flushed and sat against the tiled wall, crying again, this time only a profound sorrow fleeing my soul. She approached me and rested her head on my back from the edge.

"I apologize, Angel. This is destroying our day. We should have a fantastic time. It's a shambles."

"Bear, look at me," she said commandingly. Diana was tough when she wanted to be. I fixed my gaze on her and prepared to listen. However, first... "Wait, clean your teeth first. Sorry, but your breath stinks..." I gave a small grin and went to the sink to brush my teeth thoroughly, followed by mouthwash.

"All right, better?" As I sat next to her again, I inquired.

"Much," Diana said with a grin, gently kissing me to highlight how clean my breath was. "OK, well. First and foremost, you have little to apologize for. Your father does, but he should apologize to you and particularly to your mother. I don't think whether we go to the concert or not right now. There will be many chances for both Dead and other artists to perform. What I am concerned about is what is right for you and us. If that's what you like, I'm comfortable with only having each other all night. "All I want to do tonight is be there for you."

I kissed Diana and hugged her close. "I'd like to go tonight. I realize you've been anticipating this performance for weeks. I've done the same. I'm not going to make him destroy this for us. I have to drive you back to camp tomorrow night, and then I have to come home and deal with him. Paul Grossman is an accountant, a family man, and a cheater. But today, tonight, and tomorrow, I want to spend time with the most incredible woman I meet. My adoration. My whole being." We embraced there on the bathroom tile, still seated. I was holding her, relieved a lot of pain. At least for the day.

We gathered ourselves together and left my place. Surprisingly, we were still starving, so we went to our nearest Kosher deli and shared some hot dogs and a potato knish, as well as a pair of Dr. Brown's Diet sodas, Cream for Diana, and Black Cherry for me. (Trust me, they're the finest diet soft drinks you'll find anywhere!) Then we went into Manhattan and checked into our hotel, The Hilton on 6th and 54th, just a few blocks from Radio City Music Hall.

The remainder of the day was spent lying in bed and making love. We loved each other, which I believe was what we wanted to feel like ourselves. Diana resurrected the part of me that made me feel normal once more.

We walked the few blocks to Radio City at 6 p.m., and there was already a crowd of Dead Heads and want tobes (like Diana and me) milling around outside, two hours before the broadcast. Many young people wandered about with a single finger in the air (indicating that they just wanted one fare), and posters read 'I NEED A MIRACLE!', asking for a ticket, preferably for free. We moved a few more blocks to a coffee shop and bought something light to eat. We also had good appetites, even though we were both 18 and competitive. And we headed back in as the doors opened at 7:30 a.m.

It's a stunning Art Deco theatre from the 1930s that seats around 6,000 people and has excellent music. It's an excellent venue for a gig. We took seats at the front of the first balcony.

"Thank you so much, Bear. My very first Dead show!" Diana was thrilled, and I was overjoyed for her. Plus, I liked going to gigs, and I grew to appreciate the Grateful Dead more and more each year. Many of you who are fans will recognize what I'm referring to. Being there, particularly with Diana, was a welcome diversion.

The lights went out just after 8 p.m., and the band emerged, tuning their guitars and breaking out into Bertha, one of their favourite openers. Everyone was on their feet, even Diana, jumping at their seats and in the aisles, others high on ecstasy. When the scent of marijuana filled the house, I lit one of the three joints I had brought, puffed, and handed it to Diana. She sent me a questioning glance before taking a puff and coughing her ass off. She handed it back to me, and I struck it again, passing it on as other joints passed by. Diana took another drag before waving it off, and I was happily buzzed. It wasn't for her, but she didn't mind if I joined in.

Before taking a break, Jerry, Bob, and the guys (and Donna Jean) performed several well-known songs such as Cassidy, Row Jimmy, Deal, and Peggy-O. We stayed for a bit after the lights came on.

"They're amazing!" exclaimed my new Dead Head girlfriend as she kissed me on the lips. "I'm having a fantastic time! Except for the smoke, of course. My throat is parched. Could you please bring us anything to drink?"

"Angel, of course. You are welcome to wait here. I won't be gone far." We kissed once more, and I went to get us a fountain drink from the concession stand, packed with thirsty and hungry people. Diana gratefully sipped a long draw from the straw while I took back a big Coke with lots of colds. The second set was almost as entertaining. Dire Wolf, Fire on the Mountain, Scarlet Begonias, and Terrapin Station, all with lengthy jams, I Know You Rider, China Cat Sunflower, and a fantastic Sunshine Daydream and Stuck Inside of Mobile... finale 2 The lights came up. We filed out, a cloud of smoke lingering in the background, stinging our eyes and throats, but it didn't bother us. It was a fantastic exhibition and a fantastic time.

I placed my arm around Diana and said as we steadily made our way to the aisle stairs, "So, what do you think? Was the second collection on par with the first?"

"Much better! Except for the smoke, of course. I can't wait to get some fresh air outdoors. But, Bear, this was a fantastic moment. Thank you so much for getting me here." We wrapped our arms around each other and led the crowd before we got outside. It was a nice four-block walk to our hotel on a warm yet cool night. It also made it easy for us to relax and made our eyes feel brighter. It was late in several ways, but Midtown Manhattan never sleeps, and there was plenty of traffic with associated noises on our tour. I adored Manhattan and wished that one day I would be able to move there.

When we returned to our place, I filled a bucket of ice from the machine down the hall, and we drank from the mini-bar. We undressed, changed into some light sleepwear, and cuddled whilst watching some television. "Diana, do you mind if we just chill like this for a bit and then go to bed? I'm exhausted; it's been a busy day. And not everyone has been enjoyable."

"Jon, I'm so happy you brought it up. I believe I am still overtired. I just want to sleep next to you while holding my huge sweet Bear. We'll make up for it in the morning, right? "She inquired, optimistic.

"It will be fantastic. It's a fantastic way to start the day. particularly in your case." We kissed a couple of times and switched off the lights, keeping the television on as we cuddled. "My Angel, I adore you. Thank you for putting up with me this afternoon."

"Bear, you'll never have to thank me for that. That's why we're here: to support each other. I adore you. Almost always." She made a contented sound as she snuggled up to me. I was more concerned with my parents than I was about Diana. I had little idea how I would approach my father or even my mother without spilling the beans. Damn him for destroying our family. Diana fell asleep instantly, but it took me a long time to fall asleep.